G000114479

# COME AND RECEIVE LIGHT

Gregory Collins OSB

# Come and Receive Light
MEDITATIONS FOR MINISTERS OF CHRIST

the columba press

First published in 2003 by
the columba press
55A Spruce Avenue, Stillorgan Industrial Park,
Blackrock, Co Dublin


Cover by Bill Bolger
The cover picture is The Transfiguration by Patrick Pye
and is used by kind permission of the artist.
Origination by The Columba Press
Printed in Ireland by ColourBooks Ltd, Dublin

ISBN 1 85607 399 8

Copyright © 2003, Gregory Collins OSB

# Contents

Foreword *by Bishop Leo O'Reilly*                                    7
Introduction                                                         9

1.  Focusing on Christ                                              13
2.  Some Scriptural Principles for Prayer                           21
3.  Methods of Prayer                                               29
4.  Praying the Jesus Prayer                                        36
5.  Sin, Weakness and Conversion                                    45
6.  Living the Eucharist                                            53
7.  Deepening Prayer: A Lesson from
        the Patron Saint of Switzerland                             63
8.  To the Honour and Glory of the Trinity                         72

Postscript                                                          83

# Foreword

I am proud claim some small part in the origin of this book in the sense that it is based on talks given by Fr Gregory Collins OSB at our diocesan retreat which takes place every year in the idyllic surroundings of Dromantine Conference Centre, Co Down. When I invited Fr Gregory to give the retreat last year he expressed some reservations about the idea of a monk, who hadn't much experience of pastoral ministry, preaching to those who had. I am very happy that he accepted the invitation despite his reservations because his retreat was a tonic and was greatly appreciated by all of us who were fortunate enough to have taken part in it.

I am delighted too that Fr Gregory has decided to publish the talks he gave for the benefit of a wider readership. At a time when the shelves of bookshops are laden down with books on new age spirituality, astrology, and all kinds of spiritual self-help manuals, it is refreshing to find a book of solid spirituality rooted in the scriptures and in the Fathers of the church, but one which is also very readable and practical.

This is first and foremost a book about prayer and as such it has a message for every Christian, lay or cleric or religious of any denomination. The author is very conscious of the difficulties experienced in these times by members of the Catholic Church, and especially by priests and religious. It is a time when old certainties have been shaken, when there is disillusionment with church authorities and a loss of confidence in their leadership. Church attendances are smaller and vocations are fewer. A certain amount of despondency and lack of morale, especially among clergy is widespread. But the author sees the answer to this chaos and confusion, in the first place, not in better media management or in quick-fix pastoral strategies. Rather, he says, we need 'a contemplative vision of the mysteries of Christ and a deep union with God in the Holy Spirit'. He continues: 'Such a vision can only be founded on personal prayer, personal contact with God, as a habitual state of soul.'

So prayer is the key and, in so far as any book can tell you how to pray, this one will. It deals with methods of prayer, the scriptural principles of prayer, *lectio divina*, the Jesus Prayer, and the art of combining prayer with an active and busy life. The author draws on his Benedictine experience and frequently quotes St Benedict to good effect. He also brings a great knowledge of the Fathers of the church, especially those of the Eastern tradition, to the task. Most of all he quotes the scriptures and especially the gospels. Drawing on the spirituality of St Maximos the Confessor, he says: 'By exposing our hearts to the word of scripture we may, by God's grace, catch a glimpse of his true Word, the incarnate Lord Jesus.' Prayer must be always Christ-centred and Trinitarian.

I congratulate Fr Gregory on the publication of this book. His retreat to the clergy of Kilmore was an inspiration and I am delighted that many more will be able to share this inspiration and benefit from his wisdom and his spirituality. I warmly recommend *Come and Receive Light* to all who want to learn how to pray or to deepen their experience of prayer.

✠ *Leo O'Reilly*
*Bishop of Kilmore*

# Introduction

This book first saw the light as a series of talks given to the clergy of the Roman Catholic diocese of Kilmore in Ireland, but I hope it may also speak to anyone ministering among the people of God, whether Roman Catholic, Orthodox or Protestant. This is a time of great change in Christianity, with considerable disquiet within the church regarding issues of leadership and ministry. Much discussion and probably much reform is needed in both areas. It is likely to be a difficult and painful process when it eventually happens.

I am not a diocesan priest, and apart from working in a boarding school, hearing confessions and preaching retreats, my pastoral experience is rather limited. Therefore I will not presume to comment on an area of life in the church today about which I know very little.

But as a monk, called to search for God in community, I am committed to the structures and rhythms of monastic life as the Benedictine tradition has handed them down for 1500 years. Those structures include a life lived in stability, the daily chanting of God's praises in the liturgy of the hours, the solemn celebration of the mysteries of Christ, and frequent exposure to scripture in an atmosphere of silent prayer. The rhythms include watching the seasons of nature come and go, and living in harmony with the liturgical cycle as it re-presents the mysteries of Christ year by year. By our specific vocation, we monks are called by God to search for a state of unceasing prayer. The aim of monastic life is to gain a deeper understanding of the mysteries of Christ by the light of the Holy Spirit, so as to grasp more deeply the common vocation of all Christians: conscious union with God. In this book I will therefore speak about my monastic experience of prayer: how to carry it out, how to learn from it who God really is, and how to discern what he calls us to do in fidelity to his will. Such fidelity is demanded of all Christians, regardless of their state of life in the church. We are invited by God to hear the words the Father spoke about Jesus when he was transfigured on the mountain: 'This is my Son, the beloved; listen to him.' We are invited to realise that he speaks them to us as well, inviting us to call him, as Jesus did, 'Abba, Father.'

In the following chapters I will concentrate on some central aspects of our Christian faith and discuss how we can internalise them in prayer. These will include the call to transfiguration, the practicalities of prayer, and praying in the name of Jesus. I will look at coping with our weakness in communion with him and the importance of the eucharist in our daily lives. I will also reflect on a prayer text from the patron Saint of Switzerland (Nicholas of Flüe), using it to gain practical knowledge of what happens as the life of prayer begins to deepen.

At the end I will look at the importance of the Trinity in our vision of God and at how it should affect our understanding of the church. I am emphasising these foundational aspects of the faith not in order to evade the difficult practical issues facing the church today, but so as to highlight what is most central in the Christian life. The aim is to establish a proper focus. I believe that in order to survive at all as a Christian in the contemporary world – quite apart from struggling with the demands of ministry – it is imperative to establish a contemplative vision of the mysteries of Christ and a deep union with God in the Holy Spirit. Such a vision can only be founded on personal prayer, personal contact with God, as a habitual state of soul.

Without a contemplative vision based on prayer, our preaching is likely to be sterile, our liturgies dry and form-alistic, our pastoral outreach weak or non-existent. Without it, I believe our faith and witness must certainly perish. But with it, as St Paul says, we can do all things in God who gives us strength. St Luke in his account of the annunciation, tells us that nothing is impossible to God. We need to listen to these witnesses, and realise that once Christ's love has been truly experienced in the depths of the heart it can never fade or disappear, providing it is kept alive in prayer.

My aim in these reflections is to focus the soul's eyes on the mysteries of Christ. I want us to draw life from him, the bread of life, so as to receive help to continue the jour-ney onwards, ministering God's grace to his people. In the strength of this food we can bring him to a world which, in its deepest desire, is yearning for union with the living God.

# CHAPTER 1

# Focusing on Christ

During the celebration of the Byzantine eucharistic liturgy, at the preparation of the holy table, before the recitation of the Creed, the choir sings the *Cherubikon*, an early Christian hymn proclaiming that we carry out our worship in company with the angels. It includes the following words:

*Let us lay aside all earthly cares that we may receive the King of all, accompanied invisibly by the angelic hosts.*

Taking our cue from this magnificent eastern hymn I would suggest that the best preparation for contemplative prayer is to lay aside one's earthly cares so as to open the eyes of the heart to the coming of Jesus Christ, the Son and Word of God, made flesh for our salvation. He it is who calls us into the service of the living God, into the most intimate friendship and love with the Holy Trinity.

One of the best ways to come close to Christ is to consider the gospel accounts of his transfiguration, which tradition says occurred on Mt Thabor. On the holy mountain, shining in the full splendour of his glory, Jesus unveiled the deepest truth about himself before three of his apostles. But he also teaches us important things about ourselves as well. St Luke's account (Luke 9: 28-36) runs as follows:

*Jesus took with him Peter and John and James and went up on the mountain to pray. And while he was praying, the appearance of his face changed and his clothes became dazzling white. Suddenly they saw two men, Moses and Elijah, talking to him. They appeared in glory and were speaking of his*

*departure, which he was about to accomplish at Jerusalem.*
*Now Peter and his companions were weighed down with*
*sleep; but since they had stayed awake, they saw his glory and*
*the two men who stood with him. Peter said to Jesus, 'Master*
*it is good for us to be here; let us make three dwellings, one for*
*you, one for Moses and one for Elijah' – not knowing what he*
*said. While he was saying this, a cloud came and overshad-*
*owed them; and they were terrified as they entered the cloud.*
*Then from the cloud came a voice that said, 'This is my Son,*
*my Chosen; listen to him!' When the voice had spoken, Jesus*
*was found alone. And they kept silent and in those days told*
*no one any of the things they had seen.*

St Mark, in his description of the event, says that Jesus
called them apart precisely so that they could be alone
with him, and that the voice from heaven referred to him
as the beloved Son. More pointedly still, Mark tells us that
Jesus warned them to say nothing about what they had
seen until he had risen from the dead, a saying which dis-
turbed and perplexed them. There is scarcely a more ap-
propriate place in the whole of scripture from which to
begin considering the adventure of prayer, contemplation
and vocation.

The account of the transfiguration unveils for us the
deepest truth about Jesus, for in this vision on the holy
mountain he shows us who he really is. St John of
Damascus, commenting on this mystery, observed that in
fact nothing essential really happened to Jesus. Instead,
something happened to the apostles. They received a new
kind of sight, a new perception. The effect of the transfiguration on them was similar to the first of the signs Jesus
worked at the marriage feast at Cana in Galillee when he
turned water into wine: 'He let his glory be seen and his
disciples believed in him.'

On the mountain of Thabor, Jesus also let his glory be
seen. He drew back the veil from the apostles' eyes so that
the full truth of his divine mystery could be made manifest.

It was the glory of the Word-made-flesh, the splendour of
eternal light revealed in time. The revelation of this glory –
the fulfilment of the many glorious appearances of God in
the old covenant – is expressed with poetic power in the
ancient preface from the Christmas liturgy: 'In him we see
our God made visible, and so are caught up in love of the
God we cannot see.' The divine light shines through the
humanity of Jesus, but it was concealed by the form of the
servant characteristic of his incarnate life. On the mountain-top he opened his disciples' eyes and enabled them to
see it.

In the gospel passage, Moses and Elijah appear beside
him, pointing to him as the fulfilment of the law and
prophecies, as the manifestation of the truth for which
Israel had waited. They were the heralds of what was to
come, but Jesus is the reality. As we read in the Letter to
the Hebrews, they were obedient as servants, but Jesus is
by nature the very child of God whom all must obey. Nor
does this event only teach us who Jesus is, but also what he
came to do. Luke says that they were talking about his
Passover, his coming death and resurrection which he
would accomplish in Jerusalem. This was the driving force
of Christ's life, the primary motivation for his coming, for
as Henri de Lubac once observed, the eternal Son did not
become incarnate just to be incarnate, but so that, as the incarnate one, he could take away the sins of the world by
giving up his life on the cross. The transfiguration is the
unveiling of this mystery of reconciliation, the revelation
of God's loving will to save and transfigure all things,
through the sacrifice of his only Son.

That is why in the Letter to the Hebrews the words of
the psalmist echo in his mouth as he enters the world:
'Here I am Lord, I come to do your will!' This will of God,
the call to redemptive suffering is the chalice Jesus longed
to drink, the baptism with which he yearned to be baptised. Bathing him in the glory of God, symbolised by the
overshadowing cloud, the Father witnesses to him as his

beloved Son. Here on the mountain, all truth is revealed: the Father's loving will to save the world, the old covenant completed in the new, the incarnate Saviour on the way towards his paschal sacrifice, and the cloud of glory shining with the light of the Holy Spirit. Small wonder that Peter, stupefied by splendour, speaks as one inebriated, or out of his senses, or that in the Orthodox icons of this mystery, the apostles fall down before Jesus in fear and wonder. Whenever we lose our focus on Christ – on who he is, what he does and what he calls us to receive – we need to return to this mystery of the transfiguration. Here the light of God's glory shines, a light that darkness, whether of unbelief or cynicism, can never quench.

But in addition to what Jesus revealed to the apostles about himself, I would also suggest that this mystery reveals other important truths. Three deserve particular attention.

First, Jesus takes the apostles away to be alone with him. He draws them apart from the crowd, leading them from the plain to the top of the mountain. Traditionally, Israel met its God in two privileged types of place, the mountain and the desert. In the latter God purified his people, teaching them through hardship and homelessness to disencumber themselves of surplus baggage, and return stripped and purified to the path of his will; but on the mountain, he revealed his glory and gave the law to Moses.

The story of the transfiguration shows us that if we wish to focus properly on Christ, and come to the full knowledge of the truth about him, we must let him lead us into spaces filled with solitude. Certainly not everyone is called to become a monk in an institutional sense, but all Christians have what one might call a monastic dimension to their being – an inner thrust towards union with God in the silence and peace of contemplation. Such a thrust, planted in us by grace, is intrinsic to our nature as created beings. Through baptism it is directed specifically to the Father through Christ in the Spirit, for Christ makes his dwelling in our place of deepest desire. If it is to be actualised, we need to find personal Thabors, times and places to be alone with Jesus.

The apostles did not discern Christ's glory in the midst of the crowd, nor did they hear the Father's voice in the chaos and confusion of public ministry. God's glory is always shining, but it is concealed beneath so many veils. It is hidden behind the humility of the form Jesus assumed in his incarnation, but it is also obscured by the spiritual blindness characteristic of our human nature since the fall. In order to open the inner eye of the heart, in order to see clearly, purification is required. Ethical efforts and moral striving are not enough. More fundamentally we need to practise detachment from everyday concerns, a journey into solitude, and the opening of the soul's eyes.

The Father's voice is of course always resounding in every moment of every day, *semper et ubique*, always and everywhere. But it is easily obscured by the background noise, the many conflicting voices filling our world. An example from music may provide a helpful illustration. In classical polyphonic music it was customary for composers to build their compositions on a piece of chant known as the *cantus firmus*, perhaps some well-known hymn melody. A trained musical ear can easily recognise the fundamental sound of the *cantus firmus*, as the rich texture of voices weaves itself around it. God's voice is like the *cantus firmus* in our existence. His is the strong voice, the supporting melody we need to hear. But our inner ears are by nature dull, perhaps even deafened by the clamour that surrounds us, so that we do not *really* hear. In order to open the inner ear of the heart, in order to really hear, the silence and solitude of the mountain are essential. The great Dominican mystic John Tauler once said, 'If God would speak, you must be silent.'

Therefore, we need to go apart, or better still, let Jesus draw us apart. Time given exclusively to the things of God, such as sitting quietly in Christ's presence in the eucharist, contemplating an icon, or listening attentively to his word in scripture, is never time wasted. It is not running away from ministerial service or evading our responsibilities. On the contrary it is the absolutely indispensable condition for effective ministry. Without it, we will never fix the focus properly. We will lose our link with Jesus the Son of God, who wishes to shine on us if we are to be capable of carrying his light to others.

In silence and solitude, alone with Jesus, our attention fixed firmly on him, we rediscover the beauty of his face and rekindle the love that inspired us to follow him in the first place. When we enter such spaces for prayer, we could do no better than repeat an aspiration from the psalms: 'Do not hide your face from me for in you have I put my trust.' If we are faithful in climbing the mountain of solitude, if we go apart regularly to be with him, we will come to see his glory for he is eager to show himself to us.

The second important thing revealed by the transfiguration concerns what happens after such privileged glimpses of God's glorious presence. In post-Byzantine icons, the apostles are often shown on the left of the panel ascending the mountain with the Lord, then again on the right side, descending with him after the event. For the transfiguration was but a stage of the journey, a moment on the way to Jerusalem. In the western tradition, the painter Raphael, when he depicted this event in his last great work, went a step further. In his painting of the transfiguration, the canvas is divided into two sections. At the top we see the radiant vision of the Lord witnessed by Moses, Elijah and the apostles, but below them is a scene of great confusion, as the disciples try to deal with a possessed boy whom they were unable to exorcise.

Raphael's depiction of this story, an event Luke records

immediately after the manifestation on Mt Thabor, underlines the fact that one cannot remain permanently on the
mountain-top, but must return to the chaos and confusion
of the plain. Peter after all, had hoped to capture his trans-
figuring experience by building booths and remaining
there, but it simply could not be. These eye-witnesses of
glory had to descend for, as Pope Saint Gregory the Great
saw clearly, the life of the apostle entails a constant oscill-
ation between the glorious vision of God in solitary prayer,
and his struggle in service of the people. No Christian, and
certainly no one called to be a minister of Christ, can ever
be absolved from responsibility to return to the crowd,
where Jesus is active and operative in all his power.

We should note as well that this part of the story is
about the apostles' weakness, their inability to do very
much at all. They could only bring the problem to Jesus for
his intervention. It is striking how pastorally ineffective
the apostles often were, but in Raphael's painting at least
they do the right thing: they point upwards to the transfigured Christ, the only source of true healing.

Finally, the third important truth is represented by an
insight from St Maximos the Confessor, a great Byzantine
mystical theologian. As it concerns our way of reading
scripture it can serve to conclude this reflection and introduce the rest of our reflections. Maximos suggests that
when we take the Bible into solitude and listen attentively
to the word of God, we are doing something similar to
what the apostles did when they climbed the mountain
with Jesus. By exposing our hearts to the word of scripture
we may, by God's grace, catch a glimpse of his true Word,
the incarnate Lord Jesus. For, says Maximos, the biblical
words with their images and ideas are like the clothing of
the Word. Just as Christ's clothes suddenly shone with the
uncreated light of his divine glory, becoming dazzlingly
white, so the words of the Bible may suddenly catch fire
from the Word who clothes himself in them to speak to our

hearts. In this way Maximos relates the transfiguration to the common experience of so many Christians who encounter God regularly in the words of scripture.

Thus the time and space given to personal prayer and contemplation can become our holy mountain, where Jesus draws us apart, ready to receive the revelation of his glory. As we ascend with him, we need to lay aside those earthly cares which burden us and weigh us down – parish and other pastoral responsibilities, personal problems, anxieties and concerns about the church. Lay aside all earthly cares so as to receive Christ the Lord, the King of all! In this solitary space, silence is perhaps the most important thing, so that if God should speak, we will be ready to hear. God's gifts are never purely private. What he shows us in this time is meant to be shared with others, in the world in which we minister as ambassadors of Christ.

I began with a quotation from the Byzantine liturgy. Let me conclude with another, the one which provides the title of this book. It comes from the Orthodox service for Easter night, at the moment when the resurrection is proclaimed. We can let it guide our thoughts as we climb the mountain of the transfiguration to behold the Lord in times of solitude and silence:

*Come and receive light from the undying light
and glorify Christ who has risen from the dead.*

# CHAPTER 2

# Some Scriptural Principles for Prayer

I began by speaking about our need for solitude and going apart to seek the face of Christ so as to fix our focus on him. In this chapter I want to consider some basic principles that can guide us when we pray. In the following chapter I will discuss some of the practicalities of how to pray at all, but it is important to be clear about these principles. Much light on prayer can be gained by considering a short passage from the Letter to the Ephesians (3:14-21):

> *For this reason I bow my knees before the Father, from whom every family in heaven and on earth takes its name. I pray that according to the riches of his glory, he may grant that you may be strengthened in your inner being with power through his Spirit, and that Christ may dwell in your hearts through faith, as you are being rooted and grounded in love. I pray that you may have the power to comprehend, with all the saints, what is the breadth and length and height and depth, and to know the love of Christ that surpasses knowledge, so that you may be filled with all the fullness of God.*
>
> *Now to him who by the power at work within us is able to accomplish abundantly far more than all we can ask or imagine, to him be glory in the church and in Christ Jesus to all generations, forever and ever. Amen.*

The writer of this letter prays aloud for the Ephesians, but in doing so, he establishes in addition some important principles about prayer in general. His prayer is strongly Trinitarian. It is addressed not just to 'God' in a general way, but like the eucharistic prayers at Mass, to the Father whose paternity is the source of all fatherhood. It appeals

for the strengthening power of the Holy Spirit, and con-
centrates on the indwelling presence of Christ who lives in
the believer through faith. In addition, it stresses that love
is the foundation of the spiritual life, a love infinitely
greater than mere knowledge. It prays for the opening up
of the Ephesians so that God's fullness may fill them.
Finally, it ends with the reminder that God's power works
in them and that like God's love, it far exceeds anything
the human mind can ever imagine.

Even if this passage is not directly by St Paul, it reflects
some of his most typical interests: the fatherhood of God,
the importance of faith, the primacy of love and the sense
of God's super-abundant, overflowing, fullness of grace.
In this chapter I would like to examine more closely three
of the main ideas in the passage, as they can help us understand better what is going on when we pray.

The first is the fatherhood of God. There is no doubt
that the most distinctive aspect of the ministry of Jesus
was his overwhelming sense of a unique relationship with
God, reflected in his use of the informal and intimate term
*Abba* in addressing him. Jesus as he grew and followed
God's will, came to the awareness that God was literally
his father in a unique sense. We can see this consciousness
emerging in the story of his finding in the temple. It
reached a new level of intensity in his baptism and transfiguration, and continued even throughout the terrible
events of Gethsemene, Golgotha and the descent into hell,
when it came close to extinction. But it was confirmed and
renewed even more gloriously through his resurrection
and enthronement at the Father's right hand, after which
he revealed it, through the Holy Spirit to the church.

St Paul shows, in Galatians and Romans, that the fol-
lowers of Jesus went on using this Aramaic term *Abba*
even in a Greek-speaking environment. Thus the early
church must have viewed it as one of the most precious
treasures bequeathed her by the Lord, in the time after

Pentecost. Indeed it is intimately connected with the gift of the Holy Spirit for as Paul insists, the Spirit is the one who enables the Christian to cry, '*Abba*, Father!' Liturgical tradition has preserved this confident sense of access to God ever since. Not only do we introduce the Lord's prayer at Mass by saying that we call on God with boldness, but almost all the orations of the Roman liturgy are directed confidently to the person of the Father.

But what does it mean to pray always with the consciousness that God is our Father? What kind of quality does it impart to one's spiritual life? Here again, the human experience of the Lord should guide us. Jesus is God's child by nature, but we are children by the grace of adoption. St John's gospel says that Jesus admits us to the same relationship with the Father that he enjoys as the natural Son. That means: living daily as Jesus did in immediate dependence on God's will, accepting all things with equanimity as they issue from his hand, trusting that by his providential care the very hairs on our heads are numbered, and praying to him with great confidence in all situations of need.

In the Greek New Testament the word *parrhesia*, meaning daring or even boldness, captures the essence of Christian prayer, for in the power of the Spirit we have become beloved children in the Son. We do not only pray to and through Christ, but in him as well – to his Father, who has become our Father, his God who has become our God by grace. Securely grounded in the state of our adoptive childhood, we learn to dwell habitually in God's mysterious but supportive presence.

Mircea Eliade, the great historian of religions, once observed that in most religions of the world including Greece and India, the Father-God tends to recede into the background, giving rise to a host of mediators by means of whom the devotee tries to compensate for his absence. Nothing could be less true of the God and Father of our

Lord Jesus Christ! God's constant closeness is the kernel of the message of Jesus: there is no absent Father syndrome in the New Testament. The God revealed by Jesus is the one who rushes down the road to greet the repentant prodigal son, the one who so loved the world that he did not spare his only Son, but delivered him up for us all.

This message of the long-suffering, perpetually present Father of love must have considerable implications for how we think about God and ministry among God's people, especially if we are addressed as 'father' ourselves! For this reason we should use the word *Abba* as often as possible when we pray in the Spirit of Christ. Even if our human experience of fatherhood has not been a positive one, we retain as the psychologist Jung observed, an archetypal sense, a primordial understanding, of what a real father should be. This passage from Ephesians tells us indeed that human fatherhood is merely a shadow of real paternity, which is in God alone. Negative experiences of earthly fathers can remind us that, as Jesus expressly taught, we have only one real father and he is in heaven. Such experiences can be redeemed and healed by bringing them into relationship with God's revelation in Jesus.

We will of course also want to look at the rich feminine imagery contained in scripture and tradition on the motherly qualities of God and of Jesus himself. Perhaps more than ever, ministers of Christ need to become spiritually 'androgynous' so as to present the total reality of God's parenting of his people.

This passage from Ephesians gives particular emphasis as well to the role of the Holy Spirit in the life of prayer. Although something of a *cliche*, it is also not entirely untrue that in the history of the Latin church, the third person of the Holy Trinity has not always been accorded the central role in prayer that he deserves as Lord and giver of life. It is only in recent times that the Roman Mass has joined its Eastern counterparts in explicitly ascribing the transformation of the eucharistic gifts to the direct action of the Holy Spirit, for whose coming we implore the Father in the prayer of the *epiklesis*, before and after the consecration. But just as the Holy Spirit carries out a transforming role in the liturgy, so too he plays an indispensable part in personal prayer. There is indeed a profound similarity between public and personal prayer on this point.

The Greek and Syrian Fathers loved to dwell on this similarity between the worship Christians carry out at the altar in church, and the prayer they offer on the altar of the human heart. During the celebration of the liturgy, Christ's presence is made manifest by asking the Father to send the Holy Spirit, to transform the church's gifts. In the silence of personal prayer as well, we should offer our own *epiklesis*, asking the Father to send the Holy Spirit on the altar of our hearts that he may reveal the presence of Christ in and through us.

Jesus promised that the Holy Spirit would lead us into the complete truth, for he would take what belongs to him and declare it to us. Therefore the Spirit who is sent to us in prayer as God's gift, never arrives empty-handed. He comes laden with the grace of Christ, won for us in his death and resurrection. That is why the Holy Spirit's overflowing fullness is suggested by our traditionally speaking of his seven-fold gifts.

When we pray thus in the power of the Spirit, asking the Father to manifest the Lord Jesus in us, through the grace of the Holy Spirit, we should pray for ourselves and others, as Paul did for the Ephesians. Christians joined to the body of Christ become able, in a mysterious sense, to breathe the Holy Spirit in union with him. Again therefore, following the example of the eucharistic prayers, we should intercede not only for ourselves, but for others, pleading the sacrifice of Christ for them, asking God to strengthen and confirm their faith and love. In the Spirit's power we should ask also for many other rays of light

from the Lord and giver of life and light. We should ask for
purification from sin, enlightenment about the mysteries
of the faith, insight into the hearts of those who turn to us
for help and counsel, courage in proclaiming the message
of Christ, and prudence in knowing when to keep silence.

Perhaps especially we should ask the Paraclete, the
Consoler, to give us compassionate words of consolation
for those who come to us burdened by sickness or sin.
Depending in this way on the Spirit's gifts, abandoned to
his providential care, we learn to live each day in the
power of his guidance. It is a distinctive mark of the mature
Christian that she surrenders her life more and more gen-
erously to the guiding, illuminating power of the divine
Spirit, who becomes a kind of second soul in her.
Orthodox Christianity speaks of this as a process of becoming a 'Spirit-bearing person'.

A further aspect of this passage from Ephesians that
can help us in our prayer, is the close connection it makes
between the indwelling of Christ and the Holy Spirit in the
heart, and what the text calls the inner person. In the
Bible's Semitic worldview, the 'inner person' is synony-
mous with the heart, the word designating the centre of
the person. For the Jews, the heart was so much more than
merely the seat of the emotions or the source of the affec-
tions. It was the source also of spiritual intelligence, the
deep personal core of the self. As such, it is the point
where a human being is potentially most open to God.

When the New Testament writers want to describe the
'place', the inner locus where Christ comes to dwell, they
naturally fix it there, in this mysterious inner shrine of the
personality. The church's spiritual tradition in the east has
continued to speak about the heart, (or sometimes the
mind) in this way, as a kind of tabernacle wherein God
abides, an inner tent of meeting where he waits to unveil
his glory and reveal his presence in us. Orthodox spiritual
writers speak about guarding the heart, keeping it free

from foolish or vain ideas and images so that the divine light may shine in it.

The western tradition has used other names for this privileged locus. St Thomas for example called it the *mens*, or 'inner mind', St Francis de Sales 'the fine point of the spirit', St Teresa the 'inner room' of 'the interior castle', and the great mystics of the Rhineland, the ground, spark or 'little castle' at the centre of the soul. All these expressions signify something similar: they refer to the deepest point in ourselves, an area in each of us so deep and hidden that we scarcely know it is there.

This is the place into which the light of the Holy Spirit is poured by God at baptism. It is has been created by God, in a kind of primal grace, to be his potential dwelling-place. When Christ takes possession of this inner shrine, he comes to a throne that he himself has already prepared and made ready. For most of us, baptised in infancy, his presence is shrouded in darkness. But Christ awaits us there, concealed at the centre of the soul. He calls us to descend into this centre and meet him in a personal encounter. He wants to take possession not only of the inner castle of the self, but of our entire spirit, soul and body so that he really can become the effective centre of our lives. When we surrender to him in prayer and allow him to do this, then the heart is filled with light, with the conscious experience of love. As the text says here, it is rooted and grounded in love.

When we finally grasp that Christ is the guest concealed within us, we hear his call to turn to him. We deepen our understanding, leaving behind the superficial concerns of the upper world, the turmoil of distractions, and dive deeply into the ocean of love to find the pearl of great price located at the core of our hearts. Then God ceases to be simply a beautiful idea, or even a way of making the world intelligible. He reveals himself for what he truly is – a burning furnace of love waiting to set fire to the dry tinder of the heart. This is the adventure of prayer, the call to the inward journey of love.

Let me conclude this chapter by drawing together these insights that can guide and govern our inner lives. Prayer should be rooted and grounded in love. It leads to an experience of Christ whose indwelling presence fills the heart, the inner person, of the one who gazes on him with faith. It evokes the strengthening power of the Holy Spirit. It is the gift of the Father of love, whose one desire is that we should share fully in God's eternal and infinite plenitude of joy. Of course we cannot hope to hold these principles consciously in mind every time we pray. But they can serve as beacons, as lights along the demanding path of prayer. When it gets dark, dry or difficult, they can become an inexhaustible well of life and light for the human heart, as it struggles to keep communion with the living God.

# CHAPTER 3

# Methods of Prayer

When I talk to groups and individuals visiting the monastery, one question recurs repeatedly: 'How do you pray?' Despite the fact that those asking have usually had a Christian education and may have participated in the liturgy many times, they still have great difficulty knowing what to do in personal prayer. The question leads inevitably to a further one: is there is a method one can practise, so as to pray more easily?

In general, monastic spirituality has avoided prescribing methods or programmes for prayer. John Chapman, a famous Benedictine Abbot, once wrote 'Pray as you can, not as you can't,' and the great medieval mystic St Bernard of Clairvaux, one of the first Cistercians, advised that the best method for prayer was to be without any method! Both statements imply that if prayer is about relationship with God, then fitting it into the straitjacket of a method risks destroying its spontaneity and personal character. It might foster the illusion that one is doing something wrong by not following a particular way. It is good to keep these words at the back of our minds as we discuss prayer methods, for it is true that an encounter with the living God can never be programmed. He comes like a thief in the night, and his Spirit blows where it wills.

However, that being said, it is also worth acknowledging that some guidelines have evolved in the church's history and especially in the monastic tradition, to help people who have fixed their focus on Christ, and who opt to spend time silently searching for his presence. It is also true that spontaneity – whether that of an athlete, a musician or an acrobat – rarely comes easily. It requires training, effort and a great deal of hard work. That is why the traditional language of Christian spirituality relies heavily on Greek terms associated with physical training and gymnastics, such as *askesis* (asceticism) and *praxis* (practical effort). It is also why the Jesuit tradition since St Ignatius Loyola speaks about performing 'spiritual exercises,' a very old notion indeed, with roots deep in ancient Greek culture. Self-discipline is definitely required. *Per crucem ad lucem*: we go to the light through the cross.

What kind of spiritual exercises might be useful for us nowadays, to help us keep Christ in focus so as to live habitually in his presence? I want to describe one way, coming from the western monastic tradition, the ancient practice of *lectio divina*.

*Lectio divina* describes a style of reading developed by the earliest monks. Implicit in the Rule of St Benedict, it was handed down through the monastic spirituality of the Middle Ages, until it virtually disappeared after the Counter-Reformation in the sixteenth century. Rediscovered by monastic scholars in the twentieth century, it has in recent times achieved unprecedented popularity as a spiritual method, particularly among lay people in America and on the European continent. Its appeal lies primarily in its simplicity, the ease with which it leads to contemplative prayer, and the access it gives to the word of God in holy scripture.

The words *lectio divina* mean 'divine reading' but although this reading refers primarily to scripture, monastic tradition has generally recognised that other texts, particularly of a liturgical and poetical nature, may also become part of the process. Without denying that the Bible has a special priority in conveying God's word, it is equally true that the broad Judaeo-Christian tradition has rarely believed that God is confined exclusively to that medium. As the Jewish thinker Martin Buber once wrote, nothing may refuse to be a vehicle for the word of God. Let me describe the process involved in *lectio*, using the three traditional words used to map out its stages: *lectio*, *meditatio* and *oratio*.

The first stage is *lectio*, the reading itself. One should sit down in a quiet place, with the Bible or another text. It is important, as St Francis de Sales remarked, to approach the time of prayer in a concentrated and self-disciplined way. The section to be read should be chosen beforehand: nothing is more enervating for spiritual concentration than flicking aimlessly through a book at the last minute, looking for something relevant! In addition it is important to be discerning about what one reads. Only a great saint could find spiritual nourishment in the dietary laws in Leviticus, or the names of the tribes in the Books of Kings. First choice should probably go, as in the liturgy, to the gospels and the psalms. Also, relatively short sections are most profitably read, so as not to glut the mind with an excess of words and thereby impede simplicity of thought.

Most of us nowadays do not really know how to read with concentration. Speed-reading, constant exposure to the screen-based imagery of modern culture, and the rapidity of media information have almost killed our capacity to savour a text slowly. Our 'quick-fix' culture spells death to any kind of spiritual depth. But it was not so in the pre-modern world. There, due to the comparative rarity of books, reading was a slow, careful process. One allowed oneself to be arrested by the text, held in suspended animation before the wonders it contained.

The ancients spoke what they read, sounding the words slowly, registering them on the lips, ears and eyes, so that they simultaneously penetrated the mind. Reading was a physical act, an exercise involving the whole person, body and soul. We can learn a lot from this today because with our modern culture of reading – reading in order to have read, rather than reading for its own sake – it is almost impossible for God's word to make itself heard. Slowing down, silence, calming of the heart and engagement of the whole self in concentration on this text which mediates the word: such are the indispensable conditions for deepening one's spiritual life through *lectio divina*.

In the course of this slow, attentive reading, the second stage begins to emerge. This is *meditatio*, or as we would say, meditation. But unfortunately the word meditation in contemporary usage often designates rather complicated mental activities far removed from the simpler sense it had in the early monastic tradition. Nowadays it can cover everything from Buddhist acts of mental concentration, to Yoga, or to imaginative prayer methods in which we run 'inner videos' of the life of Christ in our heads. But meditation in the early church and in the monastic tradition was a much simpler, more accessible activity.

In monastic meditation, a few words from the text pondered in *lectio* are selected, repeated with the mouth, and turned over in the depths of the heart. The matter for meditation is thus anything but complicated. It consists of short phrases or individual words, taken from one's reading and made one's own. The psalms are a positive goldmine for such short texts, since they represent every range of need and emotion from misery to jubilation.

The early Cistercians, when they spoke about meditation, borrowed homely images from their farming experience, comparing monks who read to cows grazing in the fields. Like them, the monks should bite off short sections of nourishing grass (the word) from the field (the Bible) and chew them over, storing them within so as to extract their nutritional value. When they have finished with one mouthful, then they simply move on to another. There could hardly be a better evocation of how meditation fills the 'stomach' of the inner self with the word. Rumination, slow, attentive chewing on God's word, swallowing, regurgitating and then finally absorbing it, allows the word to penetrate and nourish the depths of the heart.

Commenting on this process, one of the desert fathers once suggested that it is a mistake to think of God's word as something hard. It only seems that way to us. But on the contrary, he says, it is the human heart that is hard. God's word, the water of life, is in fact soft, gentle and kind. But if through constant, inner meditation and repetition, we allow this soft water of the word to drip on to the hardened heart, then over many years it gradually drills an opening in the heart. Through this small crack in the stoniness of the heart, the living waters of the Spirit begin to flow until the heart is widened, and eventually opened up to God. Meditation entails frequently exposing the heart – the fundamental mission territory within us all – to the word of God that brings us light and life.

Before moving on to the third stage, *oratio*, I would like to dwell for a moment on this theme of *meditatio* as a filling of the mind and heart with short prayer texts and inspiring words from scripture. Being a way of catechising the heart, it establishes a valuable 'resource centre' in the soul. From it, words of scripture literally learnt by heart, can emerge in times of pastoral need. When hearing confessions or giving counsel for instance, it can often be the case that in the midst of feeling one's own spiritual poverty and emptiness in the face of a difficult problem, one is suddenly illuminated by a text from scripture, which had been implanted in the heart during the time of *lectio*.

The word surfaces from the depths of the heart and emerges into the mind as a source of comfort, correction, or advice. In such times, as St Paul says, we do not proclaim ourselves, but Christ Jesus. After all, as we read in the letter to the Hebrews, the word of God is a two-edged sword, capable of piercing between the joints and marrow of the soul. In the words of the prophet Isaiah, it never returns to God without carrying out what he intends it to do.

Such a fund of verses carried half-consciously in the heart, can also surface to meet one's own spiritual needs

with divine comfort and support in times of difficulty. I
once heard how this happened to a Belfast man, who had
faithfully recited the breviary for many years. In the early
1980s when he was working in a bar, masked men entered
and held him at gunpoint for several hours. Although it
later became evident that it was in fact a burglary, it looked
initially like a sectarian murder operation. This man – who
had never heard of monastic meditation – told me that in
the uncanny silence in which he sat, some words from the
91st psalm that he had recited in Compline, the night
prayer of the church,  every Sunday night for years, sur-
faced spontaneously in his mind:

> *You will not fear the terror of the night, nor the arrow that*
> *flies by day, nor the plague that prowls in the darkness, nor*
> *the scourge that lays waste at noon. A thousand may fall at*
> *your side, ten thousand fall at your right; you it will never*
> *approach, his faithfulness is buckler is shield. For you has he*
> *commanded his angels to keep you in all your ways.*

Sustained by these words, he calmly survived the night
with the confidence that God had awakened his heart to
hear these words spoken by the Spirit in him at that time.
Such an experience indicates how the word of God can
suddenly emerge from the heart to give strength and support in time of need. But it is of course necessary to place it
there through reading and meditation, if it is to do its work
when it is needed!

The third stage is *oratio*, or prayer itself. St John Cassian,
one of the earliest monastic authorities, described prayer
through a striking metaphor. He speaks of a spark of
prayer, or what he calls 'fiery prayer' suddenly darting up
to God. In another place he says that in these moments of
grace, we recite the psalms as if we had actually written
them ourselves:

> *Do not hide your face from me, for in you have I put my trust!*
> *Turn to me and have mercy, for I am lonely and poor! O God,*
> *you are my God, for you I long, for you my soul is thirsting!*

In this way, a fire of prayer is kindled in the hearth of the heart. *Meditatio* brings the raw material of God's word, which we pile on the fire, so that the flames of prayer may reach up to the presence of God. Nor should we forget that like any fire, a breeze is needed to kindle it and to keep it in existence. Russian Orthodox monastic writers compare this breeze to the breath of God, his Holy Spirit, or *Pneuma*, which he breathes out on us through the risen Christ.

One of the most valuable aspects of *lectio divina*, is its great simplicity. It calls for attention to the word of God, slow meditative repetition of the text, fixing it in the heart, then returning it to God in simple acts of thanksgiving, praise and intercession. If, in the biblical words, the heavenly Word is made flesh for us, then in *lectio divina* we give it back to God in prayer. The word becomes prayer! *Lectio* has its own gentle rhythm. When we tire of the section we are reading, or feel we have extracted all possible nourishment, then we simply move on and begin again. We are after all, always beginners in plumbing the limitless depths of God as he reveals himself to us in his word. If this method of meditative reading and gentle repetition is carefully practised with self-discipline and patience, it eventually bears spiritual fruit in us, the fruit of conscious contact with God.

We gradually develop a biblical 'culture of the heart'. The word of God generates a kind of second nature in us, making us see things according to his mind. We establish within ourselves a fund of words from God for all situations that arise, and a rich resource for preaching at the liturgy. We grow in sensitivity to what lies within the words in the pages of our Bibles and lectionaries. For the divine word is not simply that which is written on the printed page. It is the personal Word of the living God, the Word-made-flesh, Jesus our crucified and risen Lord, who pours his Spirit out upon us, in and through the word of scripture.

# CHAPTER 4

# Praying the Jesus Prayer

Many spiritual teachers in eastern and western Christianity, and indeed those belonging to other religions as well, teach that short prayers emerge spontaneously out of meditation. In this chapter I shall look at one of the most popular forms in use today, the Orthodox Jesus Prayer, for in addition to being a simple and useful method, it can help to make unceasing prayer a reality in our everyday lives.

But what does it mean to seak of 'unceasing prayer'? Although in various places in the New Testament, in St Paul and in the teaching of the Lord, we are exhorted to pray always, is this not pious hyperbole – something the dictionary defines as an exaggerated statement, not to be taken literally? Yet in the early church even before organised monasticism appeared, people were trying to take these words more seriously. Two of the greatest Patristic theologians, Origen and St Augustine, both suggested that it is indeed possible to pray without ceasing. They believed that unceasing prayer means fixing the intention of the heart on God, not only during explicit times of liturgy and personal prayer, but also in the midst of everyday activities and work. Augustine laid a special emphasis on our limitless desire for God, and recommended punctuating our daily lives with short prayers.

St Basil the Great, writing not so much for monks as for basic lay communities, laid special emphasis on trying to keep the memory of God always in mind. He taught that by training the mind to recall God's presence, a deep sensitivity to God would gradually begin to permeate the whole day. In this way, all one's activities, including such mundane tasks as eating and drinking would be carried out with the consciousness of God. But if God is to be remembered in this way, training and self-discipline are needed, for as Basil insists, in order to keep the thought of God alive, pointless fantasies, daydreaming and wandering thoughts, must be expelled from the mind.

Yet even a little experience of such spiritual practice soon demonstrates how difficult it is do this. We are by nature easily scattered, pulled this way and that by the duties pressing upon us, and the throng of images and ideas constantly arising in our minds. Attention is never easy to maintain. Simone Weil observed that we can hardly recite the Lord's Prayer a single time with full concentration, without intrusive thoughts deflecting our attention to what has been, or what is yet to come. In order to train her mind in attentiveness when saying this prayer, she would, if her thoughts began to wander, return at once to the start and begin again. Recollection is the most important activity required in order to pray with concentration. We must gather our scattered thoughts into the centre of the self, so as to focus on the presence of God.

In the Byzantine church, and especially in the deserts of Egypt, Sinai and Syria, monks who were trying to keep the memory of God as St Basil recommended, began to use short prayers as a means to help them concentrate. Many of these were simply verses from the psalms, but others were more personal and could be quite moving. One monk who had been a great sinner in the world used to call repeatedly to God, 'I have sinned as man, but do you as God have mercy!' The theological understanding revealed by this prayer is very deep. Like the Anglican Collect which begins, 'O God whose nature it is always to have mercy and forgive,' it simply states the way things are. It recognises that God being in essence love, cannot help being merciful, while we, being merely human, cannot help but call for help.

Another example of such prayer, that of St Arsenius, who abandoned a flourishing political career in Rome to become a hermit in the Egyptian desert, ran as follows: 'Lead me, Lord, in the way of salvation.' But the most popular prayer of all in the early church was the formula, *Kyrie eleison*, 'Lord have mercy,' an invocation of Christ the Lord sung hundreds of times in the Oriental liturgies. This passed also into the Roman Mass and into almost all forms of Protestant worship. With it in personal devotion often went the cry, 'Lord help me!' As St John Climacus wrote, a man on a sinking ship does not have time to compose long, rhetorical orations. He just opens his mouth and shouts 'Help!'

Eventually the name of Jesus began to be inserted into these short prayer-formulae, until after an evolution lasting centuries, the standard form of the Jesus Prayer was finally codified in Greek and Russian monasticism. In its shorter form, it consists of the words, 'Lord Jesus Christ, Son of the Living God, have mercy on me a sinner.' There are a number of other variations, including a longer form referring to the intercession of the Mother of God and the saints, but the basic form always contains an explicit invocation of the holy name, along with a plea for mercy. I have said that this prayer reached its final form in the monastic world, but it has never been an exclusively monastic prayer. Indeed today, in Greece and Russia, and within Orthodoxy as a whole, the prayer is enjoying a considerable renaissance.

Its roots are of course scriptural. In the first half of the formula it alludes to the words with which Peter confessed Christ as 'Son of the living God' in Matthew's gospel, while in the second half it recalls various passages in the gospels where people in need called upon the Lord for assistance and mercy. But as the most scriptural element is the holy name of Jesus, it is important to say something about this.

'Jesus' means 'Yahweh saves'. The name given him by the Father and communicated to us by an angel, it sums up the hope of Israel that God would save his people from their sins. At the same time it is closely coupled with the name 'Emmanuel', which declares that God is with us. Names in the ancient world were very important. When Moses asked God's name after the Lord appeared to him in the burning bush, his request was not disinterested, for the ancients thought that if you can get hold of a person's name you can in some way gain control over him! God however refused to let himself be captured by a name, instead giving Moses a form of words which was as good as no name. It is almost as obscure in translation as in the original Hebrew: 'I am who I am' or 'I will be who I will be'.

But when he sent his only Son into the world, God announced his name in triumph, for this is the only name given to us by which we may be saved. Also, as St Paul says, quoting a magnificent early Christian hymn in Philippians 2, after his exaltation God gave Jesus the name that is above all names. This name is *Kyrios*, Lord, the Greek term substituted for the unspeakable name of God. Finally, he is constituted Christ by his resurrection, that is God's anointed one, full of the Holy Spirit. Hence this formula, 'Lord Jesus Christ,' summarises the essential content of the Christian faith.

'Jesus' recalls the humanity of the Saviour, the instrument of our salvation. 'Lord' reminds us of his exalted status as the risen one, the eternal Son of the Father. 'Christ' underlines that he has been anointed by the Spirit whom he sends upon us as the radiation of his risen life. It is small wonder that the Orthodox love these titles so much, or that unlike some western writers, they rarely use the name 'Jesus' on its own. For this prayer is a marvellous synthesis of the truth about salvation. Jesus, truly divine and truly human, the Lord's anointed, the Saviour of the human race, has revealed the mercy and loving-kindness of God for all humanity.

Nor, despite the fact that the prayer is primarily addressed to Jesus, do we forget the other persons of the Trinity. For Jesus is the Son of the Father, the one to whom all prayer is ultimately directed. So too, he is the bearer of the Spirit, without whose aid, as Paul says, no one can confess Jesus as Lord. It is therefore a deeply Trinitarian prayer, enabling us to enter through the divine-humanity of Christ, into the movement of love circulating between the three divine persons. The prayer's second half takes us down from these exalted heights. Reminding us of our spiritual poverty and constant need for God's mercy, it calls for a radical honesty about what we are in God's presence, and how we stand before him: sinners in need of mercy.

The easiest way of using the Jesus prayer consists in weaving it into the daily round, pausing at times to say it explicitly but often letting it well up in moments of silence and solitude. Busy people often find this a helpful way to bring prayer into their daily work. Since it is such a short, easily remembered formula, capable of being shortened even further into such words as 'Lord Jesus Christ, have mercy on me!' it does not require much intellectual effort or the remembering of many words. Instead, directed like an arrow of love at the heart of God, piercing through the cloud separating us from him, it helps the heart to focus more easily on the presence of Christ. Anyone can use the prayer in this way.

In another way, one makes a commitment to it as a spiritual discipline. It is usually said in a seated position, with the head lowered on the chest and the eyes closed, but nothing prevents us from saying it while gazing at an icon, cross or candle. The prayers are counted on a woollen prayer rope called in Greek a *komvoschoinion*, somewhat similar in form to the western rosary. As it is essentially a form of contemplative prayer, a number of physical exercises usually accompany its use. They facilitate concentration and inner calm, so that the mind can focus attentively on the presence of Christ who lives in the heart. The Orthodox speak about finding the place of the heart, or the descent of the mind into the heart.

As we have seen, the heart is the inner shrine, the centre of the self, where the Lord Jesus sits enthroned through baptism, thanks to the presence of the Holy Spirit. Entering this shrine, keeping the senses of the soul cleansed from distracting images in readiness before God, the one who prays can touch the divine presence in a way that is deeply mysterious yet very real. For most of the time, we tend to live in our heads, relating superficially to God through images and ideas. When Orthodox spiritual writers speaks of the descent of the mind into the heart, they mean the beginning of an inner journey to the centre of the self, a descent from superficial surface consciousness, into a deep inner awareness.

Two further helps in this process are what they call the way of the heart, and the way of the breath. In the former, we search attentively for our heartbeat. Locating the physical heart is a good way of centring ourselves, because this heart of flesh is a powerful symbol for the inner spiritual heart, into which we journey for our encounter with Christ. The second, the way of the breath, entails becoming attentive to our breathing, to the inhalation and exhalation of air, which keeps us alive. This too is a powerful symbol of God's breath, his *Pneuma* coursing invisibly through all things. God breathed it into us to make us living beings, as we read in the creation narrative in Genesis.

We are usually unaware of both these physical processes unless ill health forces us to become aware of them. In this way they can powerfully symbolise our connection to

God, for although it is always there, we are usually unconscious of it. Indeed we are frequently completely oblivious
to it, except during explicit times of prayer. It is also important to note that eastern spirituality speaks about
prayer of the heart. It does not consider contemplation
primarily as 'mental prayer,' but as an activity involving
the entire person, body and soul, as these different dimensions meet and mingle in the heart.

Modern medicine has long accustomed us to recognise
the psychosomatic nature of many illnesses, especially –
and interestingly in this context – those connected with the
heart and breath! For many of us, heavily influenced by a
legacy of dualism or an excessively pseudo-spiritual attitude to life, this Orthodox understanding that the entire
person including one's body is meant to pray, can be very
good spiritual news. It reminds us that salvation is about
the healing of the whole self, body and soul.

Seated thus, calmly attentive to one's heartbeat and
breathing, one begins slowly to say the prayer. And that is
all. It is a simple method in which the most important element is concentration on the words each time one utters
them. As a technique, it is relatively easy and uncompli-
cated: that is its greatest strength. But of course, like anything worth doing, one soon learns that doing it well – that
is faithfully – is anything but easy.

The prayer requires discipline, fidelity and at times
considerable effort. A host of distracting images and ideas
crowd into the mind, deflecting attention from the words
of the prayer. How should one react to these distracting
thoughts? Evagrius, a spiritual master of the Egyptian
desert, compared them to flies as they buzz around the
head. Since trying to swat them is pointless, it is better
simply to discipline oneself to ignore them. Here, the
name of Jesus is particularly valuable, both as a focal point
for concentration, and as a shining lamp dispelling the distracting images that rise up within us.

Evagrius warned that if one follows even one of these thoughts, it can lead to complete loss of attention. Like an octopus, it may drag the mind down into a sea of distracting images. This is also true of apparently 'good' thoughts. If these are not resisted they soon involve us in an inner drama in which we are the scriptwriter, the director and the leading player. I am of course speaking here about contemplative prayer, not intercession for others. In intercession we need to think continuously about many matters. But here, the aim is to spend time alone with the Lord, focused solely on him.

What effect does the faithful practice of the Jesus Prayer eventually produce? This is always a vital question for discerning the worth of any form of prayer or spiritual method. By their fruits alone, tested over a period of time, shall we know if they really link us to the Lord, or lock us into a world of self-absorbed, illusory ideas. Any spirituality leading to a narrower vision, fanaticism, fundamentalism, or the withering of charity is never from the Lord, whose Holy Spirit leads us in the way of joy and inner freedom.

St Benedict suggested in his Rule that a widening of the heart and an experience of the unspeakable sweetness of love, are the spiritual goals for which his monks should strive. Does this kind of prayer lead to such a spiritual widening? I can of course only speak of what the tradition promises, and of my own limited experience. But I can see two principal benefits in the use of this prayer over a long period of time. The first lies in a new, more profound relationship with one's own inner depths. Regularly locating the place of the heart, entering it and spending time there with the Lord, murmuring his name and realising that he is present in the dark cloud of faith, leads to a new kind of confidence in God's providential guidance. It engenders a growing certainty of being loved by God, in a most direct and simple way.

Orthodox tradition has a wonderful Greek word for this – *plerophoria*. It signifies a state of peace, assurance and joy in the inner heart, even if in the outer sphere of life, one feels weighed down by problems and concerns. It is akin to that peace given by the Lord that the world cannot give, and to the fullness of which St Paul spoke in the passage we have seen from the Letter to the Ephesians. It leads to a state of awareness, a heightened consciousness of God, so that one realises experientially what the psalmist declared, 'I keep the Lord ever in my sight, since he is at my right hand, I shall stand firm.'

The second effect is a deepened sense of the Christian life as a process of continuous conversion, highlighted by repeating the words 'have mercy on me a sinner'. A 19th century Russian spiritual guide once said that no one should say this prayer unless he feels like the prodigal son on the way home to his father. He also warned that taking the holy name in the mouth calls for purification from futile speech. Continuing the theme of the parable of the prodigal son, he warned that the mouth that feeds on the holy name should not be content to fill itself with pig-swill!

Thus as the Jesus Prayer introduces simplicity and as-surance deeply into the heart, it also fosters an authentic feeling for repentance along with an awareness of one's constant dependence on grace. Orthodox tradition promises that through fidelity to this path, the whole of life can be-come one continuous prayer, under the direct guidance of the Holy Spirit.

# CHAPTER 5

# Sin, Weakness and Conversion

A few years ago I was discussing the Jesus prayer with a priest. He told me that while he found it a very helpful method, he had some difficulty with the second half, with the repetition of the words 'have mercy on me a sinner'. He explained that he was not denying the reality of sin, or trying to minimise its horrible effects. But having been brought up in a society obsessed with sin, he needed a more positive vision of God than the one conveyed to him by these words. Following the principle 'pray as you can, not as you can't', I advised him to substitute some other words at the end of the prayer, such as 'help me' or 'enlighten me'. But he had undoubtedly put his finger on an issue that some people today find difficult to articulate: the proper balance between repentance and a sense of one's personal worth and dignity as an adopted child of God.

It is important when considering this to let God's revealed truth guide our deliberations, otherwise we risk being at the mercy of the latest fad in psychology or our own inherited guilt complexes. Let us turn to St Paul for some light on these matters. In the Second Letter to the Corinthians (12:1-10), Paul offers us profound insights on coming to terms with one's own weakness:

*It is necessary to boast; nothing is to be gained by it, but I will go on to visions and revelations of the Lord. I know a person in Christ who fourteen years ago was caught up to the third heaven – whether in the body or out of the body I do not know; God knows – was caught up into Paradise and heard things that are not to be told, that no mortal is permitted to repeat. On behalf of such a one I will boast, but on my own behalf I will not boast, except of my weaknesses. But if I wish to boast, I will not be a fool, for I will be speaking the truth. But I refrain from it, so that no one may think better of me than what is seen in me or heard from me, even considering the exceptional character of the revelations.*

*Therefore, to keep me from being too elated, a thorn was given me in the flesh, a messenger of Satan to torment me, to keep me from being too elated. Three times I appealed to the Lord about this, that it would leave me, but he said to me, 'My grace is sufficient for you, my power is made perfect in weakness.' So, I will boast all the more gladly of my weaknesses, so that the power of Christ may dwell in me. Therefore I am content with weaknesses, insults, hardships, persecutions and calamities for the sake of Christ; for whenever I am weak, then I am strong.*

The notion of perfection as the goal of the Christian life has been so inculcated in us by years of religious formation that we are inclined to neglect the truth expressed here. We are also so accustomed to thinking of the apostles as pillars and foundations of the church, that we can easily forget, or purposely overlook, that they were always weak human beings, indecisive, ambitious or downright cowardly – even after Pentecost! The honesty of the New Testament in openly acknowledging this in so many places, has always struck me as a kind of witness to the truth of its message. That message is about God's grace alone.

In this passage Paul describes his intense religious life. It is full of contact with the Lord, closely approximating to what later tradition in the church would call mystical experience. And yet he is brought firmly down to earth with a bump. To stop him from being puffed up with pride, he has this thorn stuck in him that keeps his face placed firmly in the dust. And even worse, despite protracted prayer, he discovers that God has no intention of pulling the thorn out. By some weirdly providential design, it is actually serving God's purpose by keeping Paul humble before him.

But what about perfection? Did Jesus not tell us that we should be perfect? Has the church not set this before us as a realisable ideal, hammering the point home not only in a thousand gesticulating statues, but in religious rules, in practical instructions in monasteries and seminaries, and in pious biographies of the saints?

Perhaps we ought to remember that for a Christian, perfection is an ambiguous notion. In Paul's understanding of the gospel, which he preached in and out of season, he insisted above all on grace. Since humanity has fallen from friendship with God, only grace made manifest in Jesus Christ can save us. Christ, the new Adam, is the only truly holy one. Our Christian discipleship consists in taking sin seriously, recognising its reality in our lives and throwing ourselves on the mercy of God revealed in Christ. Therefore we must look sin squarely in the face and acknowledge our own guilt and that of the whole human race, *coram Deo*, in the presence of God, as Luther liked to say.

Yet for Paul, since we are saved by grace through faith – not through efforts of our own – sin is not the ultimate reality. Spiritual realism does not lead to gloom and despair but to the gracious God revealed in Jesus Christ.

In addition, Paul knew well, as this passage clearly attests, that nothing was more valuable in approaching Christ than the painful experience of one's own weakness, sinfulness and fragility. It is not sufficient merely to grasp this with the intellect. Our understanding must, as Newman suggested, pass from a merely notional awareness to a knowledge that is real, grounded in concrete experience and internalised through deep reflection. In this case, our weakness as it becomes apparent to us, throws us helplessly into the loving arms of God. Those arms are always open to receive us. For paradoxically, our very indigence is the quality which, like a magnet, attracts the love and mercy of God.

Only God is good by nature. Human beings participate in God's goodness, as they do in being itself, by sharing in it through grace. A healthy Christian lives therefore on a kind of spiritual knife-edge. On the one hand, we should rejoice in the goodness given us by God as his image and likeness (even if it is marred by sin) and in the even greater goodness based on our adoption by God, through the death and resurrection of his incarnate Son, and the gift of the Holy Spirit. This is the source of our dignity.

On the other hand we should continuously acknowledge that before God, we are but dust and ashes, always prone to turn our backs on him. This is the source of our misery. Yet as the psalmist sings, God knows of what we are made, he remembers that we are but dust. St Basil the Great captured this paradoxical nature of the Christian life when he declared, 'Human beings are only creatures, but they are creatures who have received the command to become divine.'

A one-sided over estimation of our own worth may foster complacency and self-congratulation, the kind of Pharisaical hypocrisy so repugnant to Jesus. It leads to pride, self-sufficiency and forgetfulness of the fact that everything we are and have is given us by grace. But too much stress on our sinfulness can itself be a denial of grace, implying that even God can do nothing for us. A healthy spirituality lives with the tension between these two poles of experience, neither puffed up by pride, nor pulled down by guilt. In both instances, the word of God offers medicine for the soul's needs. Those prone to spiritual inflation might meditate on the more humbling passages of scripture where God cuts human beings down to size. But those who feel trapped by anxiety, guilt, or even lack of self-esteem would do well to ponder the many

New Testament passages where Christ proclaims the dignity of God's children, his loving care for them and the glorious future that awaits them at the end of time.

We should seek to cultivate balance and moderation in our own selves, especially if we are expected to bring healing and comfort to others. For all of this has considerable significance for the priest's spiritual life and for his pastoral role, both in and out of the confessional. According to the mind of the church, a priest is like an icon of Christ. He reveals him not only in the celebration of the liturgy but beyond it as well, caring for the flock entrusted to him in the difficult, but also joyful occasions in which he shares the life of his people. It is Christ the good shepherd whom he is meant to represent. This shepherd was outstanding in bringing compassion to suffering people and to those with a burdened conscience. He did not break the crushed reed, nor quench the wavering flame. On the contrary he abandoned himself silently to his persecutors, receiving bitter wounds, by means of which he healed us. The Son of God is no stranger to woundedness!

Even after his glorification at Easter, Christ remains the wounded one, for he continues to bear the prints of the nails in his risen body. Indeed it was by means of these scars that the apostle Thomas was invited to overcome his doubts about him. By recognising that the one who had risen was also the one whom he had seen crushed with suffering, and that his suffering was permanently imprinted in his body, Thomas was given grace to confess Jesus as his Lord and God. He received power to follow him, as tradition says, even to the extent of becoming a martyr.

The church has therefore always laid special emphasis on Christ's wounds as the source of our salvation. At the paschal vigil we inscribe them symbolically into the candle, the sign of his risen body, praying that we may be kept and guarded by them. We celebrate also the feast of the Sacred Heart, to remind us of his pierced humanity and the wounds that healed us. St Bernard preached that through the wound in Christ's side, the torrent of divine love, the gift of the Spirit, is poured out on the world, while we gain access to the very heart of God.

The priest is therefore called to be the icon of Jesus the wounded shepherd, who because he has suffered, has the wisdom and understanding of the victim, yet without resentment. That is why, as the Letter to the Hebrews insists, he is able to be a compassionate high priest of God's religion. It is essential that his ministers try to relate their own experience as wounded human beings to the glorious wounds of Christ. We all know the ordinary human wounds afflicting everyone. But there are also other wounds, often associated with the ministerial vocation. Loneliness, sexual difficulties, fear of irrelevancy, a sense of inadequacy in living up to high ideals, problems with faith and prayer, alcoholism and frustration with authority in the church, are some of the wounds one can encounter in ministers of Christ.

Who among us could deny that, in varying measure, wounds like these appear quite often in contemporary priestly experience? Even more, who among us could deny that the wounds of the body of Christ – terrible wounds inflicted *by* her as well as on her – are painfully apparent in our own day? When we pray, we need to cry to God from the pain of these wounds. We need to uncover them before the person of Christ, gentle and humble in heart, asking him to let some beams of light, mercy and compassion, flow from his wounds to our own.

Then a wonderful light begins to dawn, the light of 2 Corinthians 12. We begin to see that our wounds are not just a painful imposition, or a heavy burden. They may instead become a path to God, and a powerful means of remaining united to him. They remind us daily that we are but fallen creatures, made of flesh and blood: but in that way they propel us into his merciful embrace. Luther, who understood these matters very well, spoke of the 'theology of the cross' and how Christ hides his gifts under the veil of opposites. There is no better way to deepen our experience of God, to realise our desperate need for grace. Yet there is nothing easy in any of this: it is about self-knowledge and that is almost always painful. It means acknowledging our own fragility, our propensity to sin, our need for grace. When St Benedict in his Rule, considers the person of the abbot, the icon of Christ the good shepherd in the monastery, he says with great insight, 'Let him always be aware of his own fragility,' and adds, 'so that he may know how to heal the wounds of others.'

This kind of self-knowledge engenders humility and is the only real source of compassion for others. Even in simply human terms, such knowledge is transforming. The German writer Thomas Mann once commented, 'It is impossible once one has recognised oneself to remain completely the same.' Such knowledge is in fact an instrument of the Holy Spirit, by means of which he reaches out and touches us and others through us. The original Greek and Latin words for wounds and woundedness, *trauma* and *vulnero*, convey a powerful truth regarding this matter. From them come words like, 'traumatic', and 'vulnerable'. If we reflect on the wounds we bear, the traumas that afflict us, in the light of Christ, we come at last to vulnerability, a kind of breaking open of the self which opens us in turn to others. Thanks to this the image of Christ – the wounded healer – begins to manifest itself in us. We become transparent to his gentle light so that others may see the face of the compassionate shepherd.

Another German writer once said, 'Pay attention to your insecurities: they open up a way to God.' The best gift priests and ministers of Christ can offer to the church today, is this gift of vulnerability coming from the knowledge of their own fragility but with a corresponding awareness that Christ, the wounded and risen one shines upon us. The way of vulnerability and self-acceptance, humility and compassion manifests the truth of Christ, who desired no status but that of a servant and saved his people on the cross. The church was born at the foot of the cross and it is never more healthy than when it stays there, its gaze fixed firmly on the Lord.

Then the priestly words of absolution, spoken by sinners over sinners, will not simply be licit and valid, but spiritually dynamic as well for they will manifest the love of the wounded Saviour coming through his wounded ministers. Sin, weakness and fragility are after all, infinitesimally small in comparison with the immensity of love in the heart of God. These thorns in our flesh are vital ones. They keep us aware that all our fruitfulness comes from the Lord alone.

# CHAPTER 6

# Living the Eucharist

As the second Vatican Council taught, the celebration of the eucharistic mystery has always been the summit and source of apostolic activity. It is the heartbeat of the Christian life. Thanks to the tradition of daily Mass, it has also been for many centuries the central act of prayer for priests who minister in the Roman rite. Yet in contemporary Ireland, Roman Catholics are seeing considerable alteration in the frequency and even possibility of celebration in some places, forced by demographic changes and the current shortage of priests. It is also generally acknowledged that despite improvements in understanding brought about by recent liturgical reforms, much still needs to be done to foster a better awareness of what this mystery really means.

Rather than thinking of the reduction in the number of celebrations as a loss, we might view it as an opportunity to improve the quality of liturgy available today. Eucharistic faith needs to deepen itself beyond the cult of the Blessed Sacrament and personal piety, to discover the deep community meaning of the Mass as the church's sacrifice and bond of unity.

However, my aim in this chapter is a more modest one. I hope to offer some insights to help deepen our understanding of the eucharist, so that it can become a real experience of prayer. I have called this chapter 'living the eucharist' in the firm belief that what we do in the celebration of the Mass has profound implications for how we live our Christian lives in general.

I shall approach this theme in two sections. The first, pertaining mostly to our personal lives, will view the celebration of the Mass as an opportunity to grow in faith, hope and love, the most important virtues in the Christian life. The second, of more social significance, will consider how an understanding of life based on the eucharist can have positive effects on our dealings with others.

Faith, hope and love, as St Paul describes them in 1 Corinthians 13, have traditionally been viewed in Latin Catholicism as the three theological virtues. 'Virtue' in this sense is a word that carries its original meaning of strength or power. These three virtues are theological powers or abilities, because they connect us directly to God. He grants them to us in the gift of the Holy Spirit, poured into our hearts at baptism and confirmation. But they are not simply given us like objects we can store away until we feel like using them. If we do not exercise them they will disappear. We need to ask God daily and even hourly, by making acts of faith and aspirations of hope and love, to activate them in us by his grace. Then they can perform the task that is distinctively their own: to keep us united to God.

Faith, the foundation of the other two, is an obscure knowledge poured into us by Christ in the Holy Spirit, giving us direct, immediate contact with God. Faith is obscure, because compared to our normal, everyday knowledge, it is dark and imprecise. The contact with God that it yields is rather like the embrace of a lover in a darkened room. It is a passionately real knowledge, of a tactile, immediate kind.

The celebration of the eucharistic mystery provides us with numerous opportunities to exercise this virtue so as to grow in our knowledge and love of God. At the heart of the eucharistic prayer, after the institution narrative, we describe what happens in the celebration as 'the mystery of faith'. These words, coming originally from the Pastoral

Epistles, were until the recent liturgical reforms attached to the consecration itself in the Latin liturgical tradition. They have now become an invitation to the assembly to proclaim the mystery of the faith. Faith is the key to the heart of the Christian mystery as it becomes present in the Mass, because faith looks beyond what can be seen to what is unseen, but even more real.

The unseen dimension consists in the various modes of presence of which the introduction to the Missal speaks. Christ is present through the Holy Spirit in his gathered people as they sing, pray and listen to the proclamation of his word, especially in the gospel. It can be difficult for priests as they begin the Mass to remember that they are standing not before a crowd, or a collection of praying individuals, but before the *ekklesia*, the called and gathered people of the Lord, the body of Christ in the world. It can be difficult too, in every hearing of the word, and even more in every homily, to remember that God is speaking, leading us into dialogue with himself.

But Christ invites us to exercise our faith, and remember that the unseen is more real than what stands or sits before our eyes. Above all, for those who preside in the assembly, it is important to recall by faith that the Lord Jesus, the good shepherd, is present in his people and to behave with reverence and respect in handling the holy gifts and leading prayer among his people.

The most spiritually effective presence is that of Christ's transfigured, risen body and blood, manifested among us in and through the signs of bread and wine. Tradition calls this the 'real presence', not as if the other modes were unreal, but because it is the most bodily, and therefore the most concrete way of being present to another person. Since the Christ who becomes present is the risen, glorified Lord, each celebration is an encounter with him as real as those we read about during the great forty days preceding his return to the Father.

Just as the apostles were called to discover new depths of relationship with Christ during that privileged period, so we should try to see each liturgical celebration and communion as privileged places of encounter. There, in the darkness of faith, but seeing and tasting the signs of bread and wine, we reach out and touch – in mystery – the Lord's very self. In every eucharist, we eat and drink with him after his resurrection: he is both the host who invites us, and the sacrificial food, which nourishes us.

For many centuries in the Roman liturgy, following a medieval custom whereby the priest recited the prologue of St John's gospel on the way back to the sacristy, this text was attached to the end of the Mass, because of its reference to the Word becoming flesh. But, remembering that the *risen* Jesus becomes bodily present at Mass, there could be no better preparation for celebrating the liturgy and receiving communion than to read regularly the gospel accounts of the appearances of the risen one. He made himself known to the disciples in the breaking of the bread, and continues to do so in the church's worship.

Simple, trusting acts of faith, give access to this presence, as St Thomas, one of the greatest theologians of the eucharist declared in a hymn: 'faith alone the true heart maketh, to behold the mystery.' Making such simple, trusting acts of faith, means inviting the Lord to fill us with his invisible presence. It means emptying ourselves of the throng of thoughts, images and ideas that crowd our minds, so as to allow the overwhelming plenitude of his presence to flow in and flood them instead.

In company with him he brings the great assembly of witnesses who concelebrate silently and invisibly in every Mass, no matter how humble the outer circumstances: the Mother of God, the saints and angels, the whole company of the redeemed, the heavenly body of Christ. To rekindle one's faith in this unseen, but luminously real world, can be a tremendous antidote to the often bleak, empirical reality in which one sometimes finds oneself in the daily life of the church. It is a reminder that, as the letter to the Hebrews puts it, our true citizenship is in heaven.

The virtue of hope is perhaps harder to maintain than that of faith, although it is a natural attitude emerging spontaneously in the human heart, even in the worst circumstances. But the hope directed towards God is much more than just a pious wish. I once heard a Methodist minister in Northern Ireland make a useful distinction between optimism and hope. The former, he said, may come and go with the winds of fortune, and is often kept up only by a certain gritting of one's teeth in the face of adversity. But the latter is founded on God's promises, on his unshakeable fidelity to the covenant made with us in Jesus Christ. As Paul says, this hope is not deceptive, because God's love has been poured into our hearts, by the Holy Spirit who has been given to us. Christian hope is grounded in the Holy Spirit.

The entire Mass is in many ways a celebration of hope since it keeps before our eyes God's saving will for all humankind. But one of the most significant places where hope finds expression is in the rites before communion. Since the restructuring of the liturgy after the Second Vatican Council, that virtue has obtained a prominent place in this section. The prayer after the Lord's prayer says it most clearly: 'Deliver us Lord from every evil, and grant us peace in our day. In your mercy keep us free from sin and protect us from all anxiety, as we wait in joyful hope for the coming of our Saviour Jesus Christ.'

Everything about this prayer invites and encourages us to stir up our hope and look to the Lord. As we prepare ourselves to welcome Christ in his holy sacrament, we look towards the end-time when he will come in his final triumph to take to himself the whole of creation. That last and greatest coming will be the perfect fulfilment of all the sacramental encounters he makes with us in every liturgical celebration.

The early church lived with the confidence that the end time had begun. Christians awaited the *parousia*, the last great coming of the Lord, his final advent. Over the centuries, this sentiment, one of the most pressing ideas in the New Testament, almost disappeared among mainstream Christian churches except in times of intense persecution, such as for example, within Russian Orthodoxy during the Soviet period. Yet the final coming of the Lord is central to our belief as Christians. We recall it, not only at every Mass (both here and in the eucharistic prayers) but in the entire season of advent, during the time of the ascension, and in the requiem liturgies we so frequently celebrate.

Each time we say this prayer at the eucharist, we should rekindle our hope in the one who is coming to judge the living and the dead. He will reward those who have, as an eastern liturgical text puts it, 'blamelessly offered the gifts'. He will sit them down at table and wait on them as he promised. Every communion is a foretaste and reminder that the one who comes today, is the one who will one day come in glory.

As with the virtue of faith, eucharistic hope is a vital antidote to the torpor and institutional paralysis in which the church can get bogged down. Each day at the altar as we welcome the epiphany of the risen Saviour in the sacramental species, we should look beyond the humble forms of the immediate celebration. We should do what the prophet Baruch commanded: 'Jerusalem, arise! Stand on the heights and see the salvation that is coming to you from God.'

Love, as St Paul taught clearly, is of course the chief of the virtues. Unlike the other two it will never cease, even in eternity. This is because, as we know from revelation, God's very being is love itself. To share in love is therefore to share mysteriously but really in God. Faith and hope conduct us to the wedding banquet, but love carries us into the heart of the Holy Trinity to be one with him. That is why love remains forever.

St Thomas Aquinas taught that through the sacramental action in the eucharist, two deeper realities are manifested. One is the Lord's glorious body itself, present through the transformation of the bread and wine. The other, the fruit of communion with him and its deepest consequence, is the unity of the church, the body of Christ in the world. This unity is charity itself, the love of God that binds us into one. The sacrament of the eucharist is given to us therefore, not just for our own private devotional needs, but for the daily building up and renewal of the church. It binds together the living stones that make up the temple of God. The mystery of love poured out in the eucharist, if it meets with obedience and faith, activates love in the hearts of those who receive it, bringing them together through charity into one body, in the unity of the Holy Spirit. The eucharist is the banquet of love, in which the divine Trinity spreads the feast and invites us to eat and drink from the fullness of love.

That is why one of the famous icons of the Orthodox Church, Rublev's depiction of the Trinity, shows the three divine persons in a circular movement of love, seated around a table on which the chalice of the eucharist is prepared. The space at the front is open, so that we can enter in, and join the feast. In every celebration of the eucharist, in the signs of his sacrifice – his body and blood sacramentally displayed upon the altar – Christ proclaims the central message of the gospel: 'God so loved the world that he gave his only Son, so that everyone who believes in him may not perish, but may have everlasting life.'

No time or place is better suited to respond in the words of the apostle Peter, 'Lord, you know that I love you', and, 'to whom shall we go?' In every celebration of the liturgy, the priest should do as Paul advised and stir up the grace that was given him through the laying on of hands. He should make an interior renewal of that original act, when lying prostrate on the ground, he offered himself in love to the Lord of love, for the service of his people. In every communion, silently in his heart, he should pronounce with love the name of Jesus, asking that the Spirit may give him strength to respond well to the many requests he will meet throughout the day. Then as St Benedict says of the monastic steward, even if he has nothing more concrete to give, he will at least be able to give a good word.

By way of conclusion I would like to focus finally not just on what we bring in faith, hope and love to the celebration of the eucharist, but on living a eucharistic life. Let us consider briefly the two most important, and inseparable aspects of the eucharist – sacrament and sacrifice – and see what implications they have for daily life and ministry.

Sacrament is the word traditionally used in western Catholicism to describe what the eastern churches refer to as the 'mysteries'. What we see and what we get in the celebration of the sacraments are not the same things. We see for instance a person being touched with water, but what really happens is an interior birth and the renewal of the person's life. We watch oil being applied to the sick, but in a hidden way the consoling Paraclete is present. So too in the Mass we see the most humble human realities, groups of people, words printed and read, song and silence, bread and wine.

But in reality, faith sees in the assembly the heavenly Jerusalem with the choirs of angels and saints. In the words and songs we hear the Word of God made flesh and the eternal song of the heavenly liturgy. In the silence we glimpse the inner repose at the heart of the Trinity. In the bread and wine we see with the eyes of faith the descent of the heavenly saviour, and the gift of his glorious body and blood. Living a eucharistic life means carrying this kind of penetrating spiritual vision out of the celebration and into the everyday world in which we live. It means fostering a sacramental sensibility, a receptivity to the unseen, the unexpected, the hidden realities that await us, concealed behind the most unlikely forms.

Such sacramental sensibility has great significance for

all forms of ministry and service; for the nuisance at the door, or the unforeseen circumstance, may well reveal a hidden grace. Training the heart through the celebration of Mass to discern the invisible presence of Christ, attunes us to his appearance beyond the liturgy. If reading the resurrection gospels is a good preparation for Mass, then Matthew chapter 25, verses 31-46, in which Christ reminds us that he hides himself in the most unexpected places, is valuable reading material for such a eucharistic way of being. Rather than just confining our liturgical understanding to the ritual celebration, living in this way deepens our sensitivity to Christ's presence in the world itself. For he did not come to save bread and wine, or to create an ecclesiastical ghetto, but to save and transfigure the universe, by opening us to his presence in the world.

Sacrifice, the other dominant aspect of the Mass, also has profound implications for living the mystery of the eucharist in daily life. The eucharistic sacrifice is primarily one of thanks and praise, as the oldest words for the Mass indicate. To live the eucharistic mystery means allowing the note of joyful thanksgiving echoing from the Mass to resound throughout the rest of life. It means bringing a spirituality of joy, thanksgiving and praise to bear, in all situations that arise. One chooses words of praise rather than condemnation, seeing all things as matter for the sacrifice of praise offered always and everywhere to God, so that everything may be for his greater glory.

St Augustine taught that sacrifice is not just something we do, an offering of something external to ourselves: rather, it is something we become and are meant to remain forever. As the third eucharistic prayer puts it, Christ, by joining us to his heavenly offering, makes us an everlasting gift to God. Our vocation – begun here, but destined to be fulfilled in eternity – is to make our lives an everlasting gift to him who gave us life, a perpetual song of thanks and praise, a liturgy of glorification.

For in heaven the sacraments shall cease, but eternal life itself will be an unending eucharist of praise and jubilation to the glory of the Father.

## CHAPTER 7

# Deepening Prayer: A Lesson from the Patron Saint of Switzerland

In a letter written on the 13th of November 1930, Edith Stein, later canonised by Pope John Paul II as St Teresa Benedicta of the Cross, advised a Dominican sister on how to harmonise her busy working day with her interior life. She quoted the famous prayer of St Nicholas of Flüe, the patron Saint of Switzerland. The prayer, well known in German-speaking lands, runs as follows:

*My Lord and my God, take from me those things which keep me from you.*

*My Lord and my God, give me those things which unite me to you.*

*My Lord and my God, take me away from myself, and give me entirely to you as your own.*

Edith Stein commented: 'These are three graces; the last is the greatest and includes the others; but take note: one must pray for it …'

Since I first encountered this prayer it has become for me a distillation of prayer itself. In these reflections I will share why I believe this to be so, and suggest some ways in which these short words of St Nicholas might guide us on our own path of prayer.

The text itself consists of three short petitions addressed to God, the brevity of which reminds us of what St Benedict says about prayer in his monastic Rule. In every-day life, he expected monastics to be people of few and sensible words, for the wise one he claimed is known by the fewness of his words. Similarly, in speaking to God, Benedict advises that prayer should be short, but filled with reverence and compunction. His advice is well illustrated in these words from St Nicholas.

The prayer is centred on the risen Christ, with each of the three petitions beginning, 'My Lord and my God'. For anyone familiar with St John's gospel, these words immediately call to mind the scene on Easter evening when the risen Christ appeared to the eleven, dispelled the doubts of Thomas, and evoked his moving exclamation, 'My Lord and my God'. Nicholas's prayer, like that of Thomas, is a cry from the heart to the risen Christ, who having passed through the deepest abyss of death and hell, is now glorified, and able to save all who call upon him. Let us consider each of the petitions in turn:

*My Lord and my God, take from me those things which keep me from you:*
This first petition is a negative one, a call to take things away. Such stripping leads to the first difficulty in the life of prayer. It is relatively easy to say inspiring things about relationship with God, but as in any relationship, it is necessary to change, and change is usually painful. It is often said that God takes us as he finds us. This is undoubtedly true. But while he takes us as he finds us, he does not simply leave us there. In a mighty Exodus, he brings us out from the Egypt of our slavery. He calls us away from our useless occupations, our construction of those secure edifices that insulate us against reality and truth. He leads us into a desert land, into a wilderness within ourselves. There he purifies us, leading us by difficult paths. He teaches us to dump the useless baggage we carry with us so as to become more free for him.

So we ask him to strip us, to remove from us those things which keep us from him. What kind of things are they? The negative ones are not very difficult to establish. Jealousy, anger, greed, hatred, lust, thirst for power, prejudice. This litany of miserable faults is an endless list we

all know well. It should never be forgotten that unless we
make a sustained attempt to identify and eradicate such
behavioural patterns in ourselves, there can be no serious
life of prayer, or even of Christianity at all. The early
monks called this aspect of life *praktike* or ethical striving.
Its chief purpose is to tackle sin and selfishness at their
source, in our desire. Depending on God's grace to cleanse
his muddied image in us, we strive so that the likeness of
Christ may shine out.

But while this personal eradication of faults is indispensable, such active work on our part is not sufficient to
reshape our lives. We are not able to reform ourselves on
our own, even with the help of 'ordinary grace', for our
efforts can only touch the surface. For lasting transformation, a deeper work of God is needed. That is why we call
on him to do the stripping, to direct his laser surgery of
love deep into our inner hearts, into the dark spaces of the
soul where as Christ taught, our evil acts originate. For
this to succeed we need to learn a new kind of activity: surrender. Giving way to God, becoming passive under his
hand, allowing him to have his way in us: this is what is
called for. So we pray, 'Take away from me those things,
which keep me from you', which means prune and pare,
cut and purge the vices from my soul.

As we pray thus, giving way to God's active work of
purification, surrendering to his work in us, a new awareness gradually begins to dawn, as self-understanding
grows. A light is kindled in the soul. An inner sense begins
to waken. We realise that the path to God is a difficult, demanding one, more difficult than we had thought. For it is
not hard to identify our grossly negative faults and even,
in some measure to amend them. But there are other, less
obvious factors impeding us in our life of prayer: our so-
called 'virtues'.

These are the very qualities by which we establish our
identity in the presence of God, the virtues we struggle so

hard to cultivate. They constitute what the writer Denys Turner called the 'ascetical personality', built up in our spiritual practice. We tend to pride ourselves – however secretly – on these virtues, because they define for us our own image of ourselves as spiritual people. In fact, without creating such an image, such a 'spiritual persona' it is doubtful if we would ever establish a living relationship with God at all.

But if we take our own image of ourselves too seriously and identify too closely with it – and we almost always do – then this very image, our 'spiritual persona' itself, becomes a barrier to deeper union with God. Inner 'wolves in sheep's clothing', such as self-congratulation on our own progress, a desire to guide and correct others, the need to reveal to others how advanced we are and most pernicious of all, the presumption that God is well within our grasp, begin to rear their ugly heads in us. St John of the Cross, following the older ancient monastic traditions, discussed these inner idols with psychological perception and quiet humour, unmasking them and teaching us how to demolish them.

So when we pray with Nicholas, 'Take away from me those things which keep me from you', we are not praying only for the elimination of the more obvious vices. Rather we are asking God to undermine our 'virtues' too, the façade we have erected, which runs the risk of hiding us, not only from him but even from ourselves. For *coram Deo*, in the presence of God, our virtues can be vices, if we ascribe them, however secretly, to ourselves. 'Lord demolish the idols,' we need to pray, 'lead us from the pit of spiritual complacency and self-congratulation, into the purifying light of truth.'

Once again, both John of the Cross and Edith Stein, have left us in no doubt about how painful such a purification can be. But without it, one remains an adolescent in the life of prayer, a spiritual *puer aeternus*, forever childish,

full of secret self-congratulation for one's own achieve-
ments rather than humble acknowledgement of God's
grace.

*My Lord and my God, give me those things, which unite me to*
*you:*
So runs the second petition of St Nicholas's prayer. What
are these things? The list is rich and varied, for all things
come from God and, used in due moderation and in accor-
dance with his will, are capable of bringing us to him. Just
to name a few in the order of creation, God's 'primal
grace': beauty, art, music, friendship, sex, food and drink.
Then, building on these, in the order of salvation: Christ
our Lord and the Holy Spirit, the word of God and the
sacraments, prayer, the Mother of God and the other
saints. However, let us select just one, coming from our
natural experience, and focus on it.

Time itself, time given us by God, awakens in us the
realisation of our own limitations. It relates us to the past
as the ever-vanishing source from which we come, the present as the world in which we live, and the future as the
horizon of our exciting, but unpredictable possibilities. We
are not finished products, but creatures in an endless
process of becoming.

This very gift of temporality, inscribed within us by
God, awakens the awareness that fragility and suffering
are built into all things. It forces us to see the transitory
nature of life, and death itself, as the horizon towards which
we move. It provokes the human heart to become a pil-
grim of the Absolute, restlessly athirst for infinity, for the
mystery of the ever-greater God, who alone can satisfy our
limitless desire to be, to know, to love. It invites the question posed by Edith Stein to Martin Heidegger: 'If we really
are thrown upon the world, then who has done the throwing?' Realisation of our finitude cuts us down to size, but
simultaneously elevates us to the frontiers of infinity. It

humbles us, preparing us to receive the power of grace through which God wishes to stretch us to infinity.

And so we pray with St Nicholas 'Give me those things, which unite me to yourself. Give me, Lord, a heightened sense of the limitations imposed by temporality, so as to find my way to the infinity of your perfection. Give me courage to embrace the contradictory crosses – the illnesses and losses, the disappointments and failures, the complexes and neuroses – through which you cross my plans and even my very self. Let me pray in the words of the psalmist, "Make us know the shortness of our life that we may gain wisdom of heart." Make me learn the lesson taught by the prophet Jeremiah: "It is good to sit in silence and wait for the Lord to save."'

*My Lord and my God, take me away from myself, and give me entirely to you as your own.*
The third and final petition is perhaps the hardest to accept. I can understand how God asks me to be detached from other things – from vice and even from apparent virtues. But how can I be detached from my very self? If I do this, what is likely to be left? Is it nothing? Can God really desire my self-annihilation, and if so why did he take the trouble to create me in the first place? It is a perplexing thought. Yet the scriptures and the church's spiritual tradition are insistent: the 'self' must be abandoned. For instance, Meister Eckhart, the famous Dominican mystic once said 'Wherever you find yourself, take leave of yourself,' and another German mystic wrote 'Nothing burns in Hell but self-will.' Edith Stein as we have seen, claimed that this third grace is the greatest one of all. Yet it raises the most difficult question: 'What is this mysterious self that I am, yet that I am called to lose?'

I have suggested already how a little suspicion of self can be a positive thing in the life of prayer. Thus we should question our very 'virtues', asking God to remove them if they impede his will. This forces us to see that who we *think* we are, and who we *really* are in God's sight, are never quite the same thing. I have further suggested that awareness of our fragility and the de-construction of our self through suffering, make us an enigma to ourselves. But I have also hinted that so far from being merely negative, these experiences are the indispensable cracks by means of which God's grace can filter through to us. God indeed prefers the cracked and broken vessel since it creates less obstacles to grace.

What does that grace gradually teach us, as the light begins to grow within the darkness of our understanding? Perhaps that we are actually, in the deepest sense, nothing, or to put it better, 'no-thing'. 'We like to think,' as T. S. Eliot put it, 'that we are sound, substantial flesh and blood.' This fiction fuels our everyday life. We like to define ourselves, to be able to grasp who we are, to have a clear and firm identity: to be a finished product, called 'I'. None of this is bad in itself, for the ego, the hard-won identity we create, is a good and necessary thing. Carl Jung observed that we spend the first half of life bringing it into being. If we did not, we would be crushed between the weight of the reality of the external world, and the unconscious forces of the soul within us.

The ego, this 'I', is our protective skin around the deeper, embryonic self. It is indeed a kind of partial self, an individual. But it is only that. The real 'I', deep within, is something infinitely more mysterious. God did not make us to be merely individuals, like chairs and tables. He made us in his image to be persons, social beings who speak, and look and love, who interact with others. If the deeper mystery of the person is to emerge, then the outer covering which is the ego must dissolve, must somehow die. It must be undermined, subverted, cracked open, revealed in all its theatrical posturing.

Such breaking down of our egocentric identity, such cracking open of our outer shell, is the painful birth in which the mystery of who we are comes forth like Lazarus emerging into light. An irreplaceable human element is involved in this emergence of the self: love and friendship are the midwives who bring it forth. An unloved, unloving human being is an individual: a person is created by love alone. We grope towards the light of love as it shines in the mystery of the human face that faces us. But it is ultimately only Jesus Christ our Lord, the face of God, who can draw us fully out of the grave of egocentric absorption, into the risen life of the true self. He alone can do this, for he alone has risen from the grave, risen into the boundless infinity of life, in perfect communion with the Father and the Holy Spirit. In baptism he opens to us the mystery of this communion.

Who, or what, this deeper self really is cannot be decided in advance, for it is not a 'thing'. It can only be suggested, through metaphors and haunting images. It is a mystery of relationship, of speaking and responding. It is a gift, to be discovered in the interchange of love with God and other people. In this, it mirrors God himself – the Holy Trinity, the primordial mystery of eternal relationships, of self-gift – whom all personal love reflects. As Edith Stein observed, this third petition, the most difficult, gives the greatest grace, but it must be prayed for.

So we ask, in the words of St Nicholas, 'Take me away from myself, and give me entirely to you as your own. Detach me, Lord, from this hard and grasping ego, this superficial outer self to which I fiercely cling, and drown it in the river of your love. Break down the barricades I build around me, as once you broke the barricades of Hell. Release the inner "I", the mystery of the hidden self, the secret person whom you know and love. Then give me totally to yourself, you who have called me into being. For you call me deeper into well-being, and beyond this life you will call me into ever-being, in the full and perfect happiness of relationship with you.

Awaken that hidden inner self, which you alone can really see and love. Stretch me to infinity. Give me entirely to yourself as your own possession, that we may be one in an eternal embrace of love. Then we shall celebrate together the unending Easter festival, in which the light of your face is the undying joy of all your saints, for you live and reign with the Father and the Holy Spirit, God forever and ever. Amen.'

# CHAPTER 8

# To the Honour and Glory of the Trinity

One of the most fruitful developments in the twentieth century church was a renewed awareness of the centrality of the Trinity in faith and life. This growth in awareness took place in both the main traditions of western Christianity, Catholic and Protestant. I am not suggesting that the reality of the Trinity was in some way absent in past centuries. After all, as the Second Vatican Council said, quoting from St Cyprian, the church is in her very essence a people brought into unity from the unity of the Father, the Son and the Holy Spirit.

Christians have always been baptised in the name of the triune God, the liturgy has always been celebrated to the glory of the Trinity, and the Creeds have long been re-cited in and out of church. But in terms of its impact on most peoples' spiritual lives, it is probably true to say that the Trinity did not play a very significant role. Yet Karl Barth claimed that the Trinity is in fact the most distinctive aspect of the Christian revelation.

In this chapter I want to emphasise the centrality of the Holy Trinity in the life of prayer, and the vital role it should play in our pastoral ministry. This will entail look-ing at three distinct but closely related dimensions: the Trinity and the work of redemption, the Trinity and the church, and the Trinity and our spiritual lives.

The New Testament proclaims that God sent his Son into the world so that we might have life through his name, and that this life is given to us in the Holy Spirit. Its perspective is Trinitarian from the very beginning.

Hence the Trinity is not simply a philosophical problem, or even worse, a mathematical formula trying to prove that three can be one. Nothing could be further from the revealed God whom Christians are called to adore. The Greek Fathers especially stressed that the Trinity cannot be discovered by human reasoning. In the strictest sense of the word, it is an absolute mystery known only through revelation. Concealed within God's unspeakable, indefinable hidden nature, it is wrapped around with darkness as with a cloud. It has been made known to us solely through the light of Christ's coming and the descent of the Holy Spirit at Pentecost. Indeed in the Byzantine rite, there is no separate feast of the Trinity, for the feast of Pentecost itself is seen as the final revelation of the mystery.

However, the word 'mystery' requires some clarification. In Christian terms, a revealed mystery is not like the mystery in a crime novel. There, if we have the patience and don't skip to the end, we eventually discover who is guilty and the mystery is solved. But in the Christian understanding of mystery, even at the very end – when we leave this world (or rather at the beginning of our heavenly existence) – the Trinity remains an eternal mystery. Since it is God himself, it is an impenetrably dark abyss, a cave we cannot penetrate, from which emanates a light that will enlighten us forever. Yet the light does not abolish the mysteriousness of the Trinity. On the contrary it highlights it even further.

One of the main reasons for this is that the Trinity is three persons united eternally in love. Even here on earth, we realise that nothing is so strange and impenetrable as another person, no matter how much we really come to know and love them! If human personality is always so mysterious we can multiply this to infinity in God.

On the other hand, the furnace of love that is the Trinity radiates light and wisdom, drawing us to itself. God does not leave us plunged in darkness but invites us to enter the circle of love in which he moves eternally. That is after all, the principal reason for the incarnation of the Word and the outpouring of the Holy Spirit: God wishes to open up his life, to let us share forever in his happiness.

At times in both Catholicism and Protestantism, a kind of impoverished theology of our redemption fostered an unbalanced spirituality and prayer. Contrary to the entire New Testament revelation, God the Father often receded into the background. With the frequent neglect also of the Holy Spirit, or worse, his relegation to the role of a prop sustaining the devotional life, Jesus became the sole centre of prayer and worship for many. Even this Jesus could be too narrowly imagined in sentimental human terms, with an over-emphasis on suffering. Worse still was the perverted notion that Jesus died to appease an angry God.

In this perspective, his role as mediator consisted in stepping between us, and this outraged deity, so that the hand of punishment aimed at us, might fall on him instead. Supported by a moral theology based on obligations and precepts and controlled by casuistry, salvation became for Catholics a tense process of keeping oneself right with God. Redemption and atonement were too narrowly conceived. For Protestants it engendered a painfully introspective self-analysis to ascertain if one was really the elected child of God: a concentration on self that was the last thing the original Reformers wished to encourage. In both traditions, gospel joy departed before the crushing weight of introspection and guilty self-consciousness.

But the good news revealed in the gospel, and the freedom based on faith preached by Paul, are very different from this tormented spirituality. He claims that what proves the love of God for us is the fact that God sent his son to die for us, even when we were still sinners. St John in his gospel says that God sent his Son into the world not for condemnation, but so that through him the world might be saved. God's all embracing desire is the salvation of the whole human race. We should hope and pray that God's vision for the world will be completely fulfilled.

Since the word 'God' in the New Testament refers almost exclusively to the Father, this establishes securely that the redemptive death of Jesus proves the Father's love for us. Also, as the letter to the Hebrews tells us, Jesus offered himself by the eternal Spirit, meaning that the third person also played a dynamic part in our redemption. So the whole Trinity is involved in our salvation.

At the baptism and transfiguration of Jesus the three persons revealed themselves working simultaneously and reciprocally. But it is in the dark event of the cross that the perfect manifestation of the Trinity occurs. A Russian Orthodox preacher once described what happened there as the crucifying love of the Father, the crucified love of the Son and the love of the Holy Spirit, poured out through the crucified one. On the cross Jesus took our place. He joined himself to us, the prodigal children, identified himself fully with us, and in himself brought us back to God. As the Son of God, bringing the love of the Father and the Holy Spirit, he came to us in our pit of sin and despair. But as the human one he returned our wounded nature to the Father who came hurrying to receive him.

The sinless Jesus, hoisting our fallen nature on the cross, assumed the guilt and sin of the whole world, identifying himself fully with the prodigal. As the Son of God become human, he entered our place of alienation and abolished the distance between the Father and us. In that union between God and humankind, the sin of the world, carved through the nails of the cross into the very flesh of the incarnate Son was plunged into the heart of the Trinity. It was burnt up by the fire of uncreated love and absolved for evermore. Issuing from that event, the Holy Spirit was sent into the world to convey to us as persons what was achieved for our nature as a whole in Christ.

Modern theologians continue to reflect searchingly on

this mystery. What, for instance, is the meaning of the frightful descent of Jesus to the dead on Holy Saturday? Might it be that God, spreading his grace to the uttermost parts of creation, filtering his light even into hearts which deny him, which refuse to emerge from their imprisonment in the darkness of atheism and unbelief, will not leave us ultimately to our own devices? Even more, what does this active involvement of the Father and the Holy Spirit in the death of Jesus through love imply about our philosophical notions that God is unchanging? Can an unchanging one, secure in immutability, protected against all emotional involvement, be a person who really loves? What kind of love could leave a person unaffected? How can the New Testament God, revealed as an overflowing well of love be an 'unmoved mover'? It is hard to reconcile such an idea with the crucified love revealed on Calvary.

The rediscovery of the Trinity's involvement in redemption has immense consequences for how we imagine God within our own inner world of prayer, and how we preach him to those entrusted to our pastoral care. Do we really pray to the Father of our Lord Jesus Christ, the tender Father, and God of all consolation? Or do we speak to some tyrannical concoction compounded in the crucible of our own souls, a mixture of negative father images from our past, confused with a philosophical notion of an unchanging being?

Do we preach a God who went to the uttermost limits to reconcile us to himself, even giving his only Son for us, or do we present a God – sometimes with great subtlety – who is a vindictive controller of behaviour, who will demand at the end his pound of flesh?

Do we proclaim that Jesus the eternal Son shared fully in our lot, in other words that he was not only true God, but also a human being like us in all things but sin, subject to temptation, learning obedience through what he suffered? Do we proclaim him as the incarnate one, so that we can look at him and know that the curtain of the mystery has been lifted a little, and that the one who sees him sees the Father?

Do we open ourselves to the Holy Spirit, as the sovereign power of God, recognising that we do nothing in prayer and preaching except by his immediate assistance? Do we realise that just as at the eucharist, the Spirit is the one who makes Christ present in response to prayer, so all our speaking to God in personal prayer is made possible only by his grace? Is he for us the Spirit of freedom, widening the heart, lifting us up through Jesus to the Father, inserting us into the exchange of love between the three divine persons? Only in the fullest understanding of the Christian faith, through a vision of redemption grounded in the triune God, the source of all reality and its final goal, can this spiritual freedom be attained. If we let this vision guide our prayer and inform our preaching, then we shall truly offer our people bread and not a stone.

But how we understand the church also needs to be influenced by our Trinitarian understanding, for there is an essential similarity between the Trinity and the people of God. For centuries in the western church an exaggerated centralisation went hand in hand with a virtual forgetting of the Trinity. For where the true vision of the Trinity – three persons united in an equality of love – retains vitality, it is impossible to hold a merely monolithic doctrine of the church. In the New Testament, and in the early tradition, the same word, *koinonia*, (communion), is employed both to describe the inner life in God that has been opened to us in Christ, and the community which bears his name, which his Spirit brings to birth. This was the original vision of the church that inspired Christians in the early centuries. It is still generally upheld in eastern Christian churches today, when they remain faithful to their roots.

Rediscovered by theological scholarship, both Protestant and Catholic in the last century, it found expression in the documents of Vatican II, as the ideal form the church should strive to attain. For in God, there is no dominating centre. Each of the three divine persons exists in a perfect relationship of love and freedom, interpenetrating one another in a mutual self-giving that both respects their uniqueness, and at the same time, relates them to one another in love. The Father has the primacy of course, as the Source and Origin of the Godhead, but he exercises it without any trace of coercion or domination, in perfect communion with the Son and Holy Spirit.

Since the church is the image of the Trinity, it is called to manifest in the world these relationships of ordered equality and respect for otherness. This fact has profound implications for how we organise the communities committed to our care, and for ecumenical relationships between churches in a divided Christendom. Do we as pastors 'govern' our people in a monolithic manner, controlling everything through power and coercion, quenching spontaneity and over-riding initiative? Or do we seek to foster a community of mutual respect, where ministry signifies discipleship not domination, where institution is subordinate to event and where hierarchy is understood as service? Of course the monolithic model is easier to operate, but we should not fool ourselves into believing that it reflects the Trinity in the world!

Almost the entire tradition of the church, from the Pauline letters to the Second Vatican Council, the liturgies, the traditions of the religious orders and the living witness of the east, are there to hammer home this point. A community meant to mirror the inner life of the Triune God must reflect this in its very structures, if it is to be an authentic witness to the truth. Love as *koinonia* should show the world that the Christian community is the image of the Trinity. Translating such a Trinitarian vision into action is demanding. It calls for constant conversion. But without it the church will inevitably become a monolithic institution composed of individuals, rather than a community of persons grounded in Trinitarian love.

A church based on the Trinity is more than just a theological idea or abstract concept. It is the living manifestation of God. Of course this ideal can never be finally realised on this side of eternity. Here as elsewhere in the spiritual life, realism is demanded. But we must not lose sight of the ideal, nor of God's ability to manifest it. Even in this broken and fragmentary world, when people really believe and entrust themselves to transforming, Trinitarian grace, the church can come to mirror its heavenly source more fully.

At the root of all conversion, as Newman liked to emphasise, lies prayer. So as I conclude this reflection I want to bring us back again to where we started, on the mountain of the Transfiguration. To become a people of the Trinity we must let the Trinity take possession of our hearts. Only if we internalise communion with the Holy Trinity in personal prayer and meditation, in adoring silence and eager receptivity to the word, will we receive light from the light of Christ, and become a source of light to others. In the adventure of prayer, in time spent apart on the mountain, we enter the space between Jesus and the Father, that space where he issues eternally from God, and turns continuously back to him.

Or to put it more accurately: we abandon ourselves to the current of love which is the Holy Spirit, allowing him to sweep us away into the infinite ocean of God's immeasurable love. For the Spirit crosses the space between the Father and the Son, uniting them in their eternal mutual embrace.

To help us pray in a more Trinitarian way, we might use the concluding doxology of the eucharistic prayer in the Roman Mass. As the culminating point of liturgical prayer, it represents a kind of summary of the church's oldest and deepest wisdom in relation to the Trinity. We should say it often outside Mass, to fuse prayer and daily life with the church's sacrifice of praise. In thinking about this doxology, an idea found in the writings of St Basil the Great may be helpful.

Basil described three possible ways of relating to God, which he called: that of the slave, that of the servant, and that of the adopted child.

When we pray the words *through him* our prayer is that of the ransomed slave, bought back by Christ's sacrifice from the power of sin and death. This is the most basic level of the Christian life. We go *through* him, because Christ's divine-humanity is the medium through which God appears to us and draws us to himself. It is the first stage of a redeemed existence. We cannot save ourselves by anything in our own power, but simply receive everything as God's gift, given us through faith in Christ. This is the state of the justified sinner whose only reliance is on Christ and his grace.

When we pray *with him* we are lifted up to another level, that of the faithful servant of God, seeking to do his will in union with Christ. We stand beside Christ as our brother. This is the state of progressive sanctification. Through faith, prayer and self-discipline we work with God (always under the action of his grace!) to allow him to bring forth in us the fruits of holiness.

But when we pray *in him,* we have realised that state of transfiguration, of spiritual freedom, in which we are inserted by grace into Christ's natural relationship to the Father. In baptism we have become adopted children, heirs by grace to all the privileges that Jesus enjoys by nature. When we consciously realise this we take hold of our baptismal birthright. This is the deepest grace for a Christian, the state proclaimed by Paul and John as the fulfilment of our vocation. We are not simply *under* the Son of God, or even *beside* him. Rather we stand *in* him. We enter a face-to-face relationship with the Father who looks with love on the face of his beloved child, Jesus the Lord, and in him on us, his adopted children.

The doxology specifies that this grace comes about *in the unity of the Holy Spirit.* Scholars once debated if this unity is the work that the Spirit performs eternally in the inner life of the Trinity as he moves between the Father and the Son, or the unity he brings about between persons in the church. In truth it is really both – or rather, the first is the basis of the second. For the Spirit of unity issuing from God, becomes the bond of unity that gathers and sustains the church. He is the one who joins us to Christ and in him to one other. Inserted into Christ, he enables us to face the Father, as he cries out in us 'Abba, Father!

Then at the conclusion of the doxology, we ascribe to God the Father that honour and glory which are his alone by right. Sealing the prayer with the great 'amen', we pray that this insertion into God's inner life may be confirmed in us. For to live in the closest possible union with the divine Trinity is to enter already the eternal happiness to which we are called in faith. It is to realise the church's goal in the unity of prayer and life. It is to be caught up into the Trinity's eternal embrace.

# Postscript

This book began on the mountain of the transfiguration. Having laid aside our worldly cares and fixed our gaze firmly on Christ the Lord, we began by exploring some basic principles that might help to ground our prayer. We then looked at practical methods to help us persevere in it. We kept the focus on Christ, by discussing prayer using his holy name, then considered how our weakness can be a special mode of access to his wounded but risen presence. We meditated on living the eucharist, not only in the celebration of the liturgy but beyond it in the personal liturgy of faith, hope and love. We sought help from St Nicholas of Flüe on the journey into deeper communion with God. We tried finally to bind these themes together in a vision of the Trinity in salvation, in the church and in personal prayer.

However, as we see in the conclusion to the story of the transfiguration, no permanent dwelling place can be established on the mountain top before our final passage through death into everlasting life. Jesus told the apostles that he had to descend again to the multitude and take the road to Jerusalem, to accomplish his Paschal sacrifice. There is no transfiguration without the humble path of obedience to God's will in the work which he assigns us, no transfiguration without the cross. Easter alone is the final and definitive transfiguration. In the difficult, demanding task of discipleship, keeping the focus fixed on Christ is never easy: but love will always seek to return to him. In conclusion, let us look at one scene from the New Testament where Christ's love for his ministers shines out with perfect clarity.

For anyone engaged in ministry among the people of God, it is a worthwhile exercise to read frequently the twenty-first chapter of St John's gospel and consider the poignant scene depicted there. In the stillness of the morning, having eaten breakfast with the apostles, the risen Jesus asked Peter three times if he loved him, before commissioning him to feed his flock. We have seen how Thomas recognised the risen one on Easter night as the wounded one, who bears forever the scars of his passion. But in this scene, a deeper wound, the soul's wound, is uncovered. There is possibly no greater image of vulnerabitiy and no more tangible proof of the real humanity of Jesus in the whole of the New Testament, than this touching scene. Without recrimination or reproach, he reminds Peter of that terrible night of betrayal. 'Do you love me?' he asks him, not once but three times, giving Peter the opportunity to heal the threefold wound he had inflicted on him.

Tradition calls Peter 'Prince of the Apostles' and the rock on which the church was founded. This is certainly a scene of commissioning, as Peter is commanded in the simplest of words: 'Look after my sheep.' But we must never forget that this office and authority in the church was conferred on him in such a raw moment of vulnerability and forgiveness. We are far from triumphalism here!

Read this passage too in deep stillness and concentration. Let the Lord speak the same words he addressed to Peter: 'Do you love me?' If you can answer, as he did, 'Yes Lord, you know that I love you,' then you will hear the pastoral charge that Jesus put to Peter, and that he once put to you as well. That charge is: 'Feed my sheep.' If you can answer again, as you did at your first commissioning, 'Here I am,' then Christ confers on you the shepherd's task afresh. He says to you: 'Come and receive light from my undying light.'

To him, the risen Saviour, the light of the world, who calls us out of darkness into his own wonderful light –

sending us to dispel the darkness of the night – be all glory with the Father and the Holy Spirit, now and through endless ages. Amen.